Burt Franklin Research & Source Works Series #150

THE SPENSER SOCIETY #1

THE

PROVERBS

AND

EPIGRAMS

OF

JOHN HEYWOOD

(A.D. 1562).

THE

PROVERBS

AND

EPIGRAMS

OF

JOHN HEYWOOD

(A.D. 1562).

REPRINTED FROM THE ORIGINAL (1562) EDITION, AND
COLLATED WITH THE SECOND (1566) EDITION;
WITH AN
APPENDIX OF VARIATIONS.

Burt Franklin Research & Source Works Series #150

THE SPENSER SOCIETY #1

BURT FRANKLIN
NEW YORK

Published By
BURT FRANKLIN
235 East 44th St.
New York, N.Y. 10017

ORIGINALLY PUBLISHED
SPENSER SOCIETY: 1867
Reprinted New York 1967

Printed in U.S.A.

NOTICE.

BOTH of the Editions of this Work which have been employed for the prefent Reprint are in 𝔅𝔩𝔞𝔠𝔨 𝔏𝔢𝔱𝔱𝔢𝔯. In accordance however with the terms of the original Profpectus iffued by the SPENSER SOCIETY, and influenced by confiderations of uniformity and convenience, Roman Type is here ufed.

A Gloffary to the prefent Volume has been prepared, and is in MS.; but the Council, hoping ultimately to place the *complete* Works of John Heywood in the hands of the Members, have decided upon deferring its iffue until it can be given, enlarged fo as to comprehend the whole of his Works, with the laft Volume, when they purpofe that it fhall be preceded by a full Biographical and Bibliographical Account of the Author and his Writings.

OCTOBER, 1867.

John Heywoodes woorkes.

℈ A dialogue conteynyng the

number of the effectuall prouerbes in
the Englishe tounge, compact in
a matter concernynge
two maner of ma=
ryages.
With one hundred of Epigrammes: and
thrée hundred of Epigrammes
vpon thrée hundred, pro=
uerbes: and a fifth
hundred of E=
pigrams.
Wherunto are now newly added
a syxt hundred of Epigrams
by the sayde John
Heywood.

♣

LONDINI.
ANNO christi.
1562.

𝕿𝖍𝖊. í. 𝖈𝖍𝖆𝖕𝖙𝖊𝖗.

OF mine acquayntance a certaine yong man
(Beyng a reſorter to me now and than)
Reſorted lately, ſhowyng him ſelfe to bée
Deſyrous to talke at length alone with me.
And as we for this, a méete place had woon,
With this olde prouerbe, this yong man begon.
    Who ſo that knew, what wolde be dere,
Should neede be a marchant but one yeere.
Though it (quoth he) thing impoſſible bée,
The full ſequele of preſent things to foreſée:
Yet doth this prouerbe prouoke euery man
Politykely (as man poſſible can)
In things to come after to caſt eie before,
To caſte out or kepe in things for fore ſtore.
As the prouiſion maie ſéeme most profytable,
And the commoditée moſt commendable.
Into this conſyderacion I am wrought
By two thyngis, whiche fortune to hands hath brought.
Two women I know, of whiche twayne the tone
Is a mayde of flowryng age, a goodly one.
Thother a wydow, who ſo many yeres beares,
That all hir whiteneſſe lythe in hir whyte heares.
This mayde hath fréendis ryche, but riches hath ſhee none,
Nor none can hir handes geat to lieue vpon.
This wydow is very ryche, and hir fréendis bare,
And both theſe, for loue to wed with me fond are.
And both would I wed, the better and the wurs.
The tone for hir perſon, the tother for her purs.
They woo not my ſubſtance, but my ſelfe they wooe.
Goodes haue I none and ſmall good can I dooe.
On this poore maid hir riche fréendis I cléerely know,
(So ſhe wed where they wyll) great gyfts will beſtow,

A ij   But

But with them all I am ſo far from fauer,
That ſhe ſhall ſure haue no grote if I haue her.
And I ſhall haue as lyttle all my fréendis ſwere,
Except I folow them, to wedde els where.
The poore fréendis of this ryche wydow beare no ſway,
But wed hir and wyn' welth. whan I wyll I may.
Nowe whiche of theſe twayne is lyke to be dereſt
In payn ·or pleaſure to ſticke to me nereſt,
The depth of all doubtes with you to conſyther,
The fence of the ſayde prouerbe ſendth me hyther.
The beſt bargayne of both quickly to haue ſkande,
For one of them thinke I to make out of hande.

The. ii. chapiter.

FRende (quoth I) welcome, and with right good will,
I will as I can, your will herein fulfyll.
And two thinges I ſée in you, that ſhew you wyſe,
Firſt in weddyng ere ye wed, to aſke aduyſe.
·The feconde, your yeres beyng yong it apéeres,
Ye regarde yet good prouerbes of olde ferne yéeres.
And as ye grounde your tale vpon one of them,
Furniſhe we this tale with euerychone of them.
Suche as may fytly fall in mynde to diſpoſe.
Agréed (quoth he) Then (quoth I) firſt this diſcloſe.
Haue you to this old wydow, or this yong mayde,
Any woordis of aſſurance er this time ſayde?
Nay in good faith ſaide he. Well than (ſaide I)
I wyll be playne with you, and may honeſtly.
And plainely to ſpeake, I lyke you (as I ſayde)
In two fore tolde thynges, but a thirde haue I wayde,
Not ſo much to be lyked, as I can déeme,
Whiche is in your weddyng your haſte ſo extréeme.

The beſt or woorſt thing to man for this lyfe,
Is good or yll chooſyng his good or yll wyfe.

I

4

I meane not onely of body good or bad,
But of all thinges meete or vnmeete to be had,
Such as at any time by any meane may
Betweene man and wife, loue encreaſe or decay.
Where this grounde in any hed, grauely grateth,
All firie haſt to wed, it ſoone rebateth.
Som thingis that prouoke young men to wed in haſte,
Show after weddyng, that haſt maketh waſte.
Whan time hath tournd white ſurger to white ſalte,
Than ſuche folke ſee, ſoft fire maketh ſweete malte.
And that deliberacion doth men aſſiſt
Before they wed to beware of had I wiſt.
And than their timely weddyng doth clere appere,
That they were earely vp, and neuer the nere.
And ones their haſtie heate a littell controlde,
Than perceiue they well, hotte loue ſoone colde.
And whan haſty witleſſe mirth is mated weele,
Good to be mery and wiſe, they thinke and feele.
Haſte in weddyng ſom man thinkth his owne auayle.
Whan haſte proueth a rod made for his owne tayle.
And whan he is well beaten with his owne rod,
Than ſeeth he haſt and wiſdome thingis far od.
And that in all, or moſt thingis, wiſht at neede,
Moſte times he ſeeth, the more haſte the leſſe ſpeede.
In les thingis then weddyng, haſt ſhowth haſtie mans ſo,
So that the haſty man neuer wanteth wo.
Theſe ſage ſayd ſawes if ye take ſo profounde,
As ye take that, by which ye tooke your grounde,
Than finde ye grounded cauſe by theſe now here told,
In haſt to weddyng your haſt to withhold.
And though they ſeeme wiues for you neuer ſo fit,
Yet let not harmfull haſt ſo far out ren your wit,
But that ye harke to here all the whole ſume,
That may pleaſe or diſpleaſe you in time to come.

A iij   Thus

5

Thus by thefe leffons ye may learne good cheape,
In weddyng and al thing, to looke or ye leape.
Ye haue euen now well ouerlookt me (quoth he)
And lept very nie me to. For I agree,
That thefe fage fayings dooe weightily way
Againft haft in all thing, but I am at bay.
By other parables of like weightie weight,
Which haft me to weddyng, as ye fhall here ftreight.

The. iij. chapter.

HE that will not whan he may,
   Whan he would, he fhall haue nay.
Beautie or riches the tone of the twayne
Now may I choofe, and whiche me lift obtaine.
And if we determine me, this mayde to take,
And then tract of time traine her me to forfake:
Than my beautifull mariage lithe in the dike,
And neuer for beautie, fhall I wedde the like.
Now if we awarde me this widowe to wedde.
And that I driue of time till time, fhe be dedde,
Than farewell riches, the fat is in the fire,
And neuer fhall I to like riches afpire.
And a thoufand folde would it greue me more,
That fhe in my faute fhould die one houre before,
Than one minute after. than hafte muft prouoke,
Whan the pigge is proferd to holde vp the poke.
Whan the funne fhinth make hay. whiche is to fay.
Take time whan time comth, left time fteale away.
And one good leffon to this purpofe I pike
From the fmithis forge, whan thyron is hot ftrike.
The fure fea man feeth, the tide tarieth no man.
And long delayes or abfence fomwhat to fkan.
Sens that that one will not, on other will,
Delaies in woers muft needes their fpeede fpill.

And

6

And touchyng abſence, the full accompte wo ſomth.
Shall ſee, as faſt as one goth an other comthe.
Time is tickell. and out of ſight out of minde.
Than catche and holde while I may, faſt binde faſt finde.
Blame me not to haſte, for feare mine eie be blerde.
And therby the fat cleane flit fro my berde.
Where wooers hoppe in and out, long time may bryng
Him that hoppeth beſt, at laſt to haue the ryng.
I hoppyng without for a ryng of a ruſhe.
And while I at length debate and beate the buſhe,
There ſhall ſteppe in other men, and catche the burdes,
And by long time loſt in many vayne wurdes.
Betwene theſe two wiues, make ſlouth ſpede confound
While betweene two ſtooles, my tayle go to grounde.
By this, ſens we ſee ſlouth muſt bréede a ſcab,
Beſt ſticke to the tone out of hand, hab or nab.
Thus all your prouerbs inueying againſt haſte,
Be anſwerd with prouerbs plaine and promptly plaſte.
Wherby, to purpoſe all this no further fits,
But to ſhew, ſo many heds ſo many wits.
Whiche ſhewe as ſurely in all that they all tell,
That in my weddyng I may euen as well
Tary to long, and therby come to late,
As come to ſoone by haſt in any rate.
And proue this prouerbe, as the woordes therof go,
Haſte or ſlouth herein woorke nother welth nor wo.
Be it far or nie, weddyng is deſteny,
And hangyng likewiſe, ſaith that prouerbe, ſaid I.
Than wed or hang (quoth he) what helpth in the whole
To haſt or hang aloof, happy man happy dole.
Ye deale this dole (quoth I) out at a wrong dur.
For deſteny in this caſe doth not ſo ſtur
Againſt mans indeuour, but man may direct
His will, fore prouiſion to worke or neglect.

                                                    But

7

But to ſhew that quick wedding may bryng good ſpeede,
Somwhat to purpoſe, your prouerbs proue in deede.
Howbeit, whether they counterpayſe or out way
The prouerbes, which I before them did lay,
The triall therof we will lay a water.
Till we trie more. For triyng of which mater
Declare all commodites ye can deuiſe,
That by thoſe two weddingis to you can riſe.

The. iiij. Chapter.

I Wyll (quoth he) in bothe theſe caſes ſtreight ſhow,
What thingis (as I think) to me by them will grow.
And where my loue began, there begin will I.
With this mayde, the peece pereleſſe in mine eie.
Whom I ſo fauour, and ſhe ſo fauourth me,
That half a death to vs a ſonder to be.
Affection eche to other doth vs ſo moue,
That welny without foode, we coulde liue by loue.
For be I right ſad, or right ſicke, from hir ſight,
Her preſence abſenteth all maladies quight.
Whiche ſeen, and that the great ground in mariage
Standth vpon likyng the parties perſonage,
And than of olde prouerbes in opening the packe,
One ſhewth me openly in loue is no lacke.
No lacke of likyng, but lacke of liuyng, •
May lacke in loue (quoth I) and breede ill cheeuyng.
Well as to that (ſayde he) harke this othyng.
What time I lacke not hir, I lacke nothyng.
But though we haue nought, nor nought we can geat,
God neuer ſendth mouth, but he ſendeth meat.
And a hard beginnyng makth a good endyng.
In ſpace comth grace, and this further amendyng.
Seldome comth the better, and like will to like.
God ſendth colde after clothes. and this I pike.

She,

8

She, by lacke of ſubſtance ſéemyng but a ſparke,
Steynth yet the ſtouteſt, For a leg of a larke
Is better than is the body of a kyght.
And home is homely, though it be poore in ſyght.
Theſe prouerbs for this parte ſhew ſuche a flouriſhe,
And than this partie dooth delyte ſo nouriſhe.
That muche is my bowe bent to ſhoote at theſe marks,
And kyll feare, when the ſky falth we ſhall haue larks.
All perils that fall maie, who fearth they fall ſhall,
Shall ſo feare all thyng, that he ſhall let fall all,
And be more fraid then hurt, if the thinges were doone.
Feare may force a man to caſt beyonde the moone.
Who hopeth in Gods helpe, his helpe can not ſtarte:
Nothing is impoſſible to a willyng hart,
And will maie wyn my herte, herein to conſent,
To take all thinges as it comth, and be content.
And here is (q' he) in mariyng of this mayde,
For courage and commoditée all mine ayde.
Well ſayde (ſaied I) but a whyle kepe we in quenche,
All this caſe, as touchyng this poore yonge wenche.
And nowe declare your whole conſideracion,
What maner thinges draw your imaginacion,
Toward your weddyng of this wydow riche and olde.
That ſhall ye (q' he) out of hande haue tolde.

The. vi. chapiter.

THis wydowe beyng foule, and of fauour yll,
In good behauour can very good ſkyll.
Pleaſantly ſpoken, and a very good wyt,
And at hir table, whan we together ſyt,
I am well ſerued, we fare of the beſt.
The meate good and holſome and holſomly dreſt.
Swéete and ſofte lodgeyng, and therof great ſhyfte.
This felte and ſéene, with all implementes of thrifte,

B   Of

9

Of plate and money ſuche cupḃoordes and coffers,
And that without peyne I maie win theſe profers,
Than couetyſe bearyng Uenus bargayne backe,
Praiſyng this bargayne ſaith, better leaue then lacke.
And gredineſſe, to drawe deſyre to hir lore,
Saieth, that the wiſe man ſaieth, ſtore is no ſore.
Who hath many peaſe maie put the mo in the pot.
Of two yls, chooſe the leaſt whyle choyſe lyth in lot.
Sens lacke is an yll, as yll as man may haue,
To prouyde for the woorſt, whyle the beſt it ſelfe ſaue.
Reſtie welth wylth me this wydow to wyn,
To let the world wag, and take mine eaſe in mine in.
He muſt néedes ſwym, that is holde vp by the chyn.
He laughth that wynth. And this thréede fyner to ſpyn,
Maïſter promocion ſaieth, make this ſubſtance ſure,
If ryches bryng ones portly countenance in vre,
Than ſhalt thou rule the roſte all rounde about.
And better to rule, than be ruled by the rout.
It is ſaide be it better be it wurs,
Dooe ye after him that beareth the purs.
Thus be I by this, ones *le ſenior de graunde*,
Many that commaunded me, I ſhall commaunde.
And alſo I ſhall to reueng former hurtis,
Hold their noſes to grinſtone, and ſyt on theyr ſkurtis,
That erſt ſate on mine. And riches maie make
Fréends many waies. Thus better to geue then take.
And to make carnall appetite content,
Reaſon laboreth wyll, to wyn wyls conſent,
To take lacke of beautie but as an eye ſore.
The fayre and the foule, by darke are lyke ſtore.
When all candels be out, all cats be grey,
All thingis are then of one colour, as who ſey.
And this prouerbe ſaith, for quenching hot deſyre,
Foule water as ſoone as fayre, will quenche hot fyre.

Where

10

Where gyftis be geuen fréely, eſt weſt north or ſouth,
No man ought to looke a geuen hors in the mouth.
And though hir mouth be foule, ſhe hath a fayre tayle.
I conſtre this text, as is moſte my auayle.
In want of white téeth and yelow héares to beholde,
She flouriſheth in white ſiluer and yelow golde.
What though ſhe be toothleſſe, and balde as a coote ?
Her ſubſtaunce is ſhoote anker, wherat I ſhoote.
Take a peyne for a pleaſure all wyſe men can.
What, hungry dogges will eate durty puddyngs man.
And here I conclude (quoth he) all that I knowe
By this olde widow, what good to me maie growe.

The. vi. chapiter.

YE haue (quoth I) in theſe concluſions founde
  Sundrie thinges, that veray ſauerly founde,
And bothe theſe longe caſes, beyng well vewde,
In one short queſtion, we maie well inclewde,
Whiche is, whether beſt or wurſt be to be ledde
With riches, without loue or beautie, to wedde :
Or with beautie without richeſſe for loue.
This queſtion (quoth he) inquerth all that I moue.
It dooth ſo (ſaid I) and is néerely couched.
But thanſwere will not ſo breuely be touched.
And your ſelfe, to length it, taketh direct trade.
For to all reaſons, that I haue yet made,
Ye ſéeme more to ſéeke reaſons how to contende,
Than to the councell of myne to condiſcende.
And to be playne, as I muſt with mi frende,
I perfectly féele euen at my fyngers ende.
So harde is your hande ſet on your halfpeny,
That my reaſonyng your reaſon ſetteth nought by.
But reaſon for reaſon, ye ſo ſtyfly lay,
By prouerbe for prouerbe, that with you do way,

B ij   That

That reaſon onely ſhall herein nought moue you.
To here more then ſpeake. wherfore I wyll proue you,
With reaſon, aſſiſted by experience.
Whiche my ſelfe ſawe, not long ſens nor far hence.
In a matter ſo lyke this faſhond in frame,
That none can be lyker, it ſéemeth euen the ſame,
And in the ſame, as your ſelfe ſhall eſpy
Eche ſentence ſoothed with a prouerbe welny.
And at ende of the ſame, ye ſhall cléerely ſée
How this ſhorte queſtion ſhortly anſwerd may béc.
Ye mary (quoth he) nowe ye ſhoote nie the pricke.
Practyſe in all, aboue all toucheth the quicke.
Proofe vppon practiſe, muſt take holde more ſure,
Than any reaſonyng by geſſe can procure.
If ye bryng practiſe in place, without fablyng,
I wyll banyſh both haſte and buſy bablyng.
And yet that promiſe to perfourme is mickell,
For in this caſe my toung muſt oft tickell.
Ye know well it is, as telth vs this olde tale,
Méete, that a man be at his owne brydale.
If he wyue well (quoth I) méete and good it were.
Or els as good for him an other were there.
But for this your bridale I meane not in it,
That ſcilence ſhall ſuſpend your ſpeeche euery whyt.
But in theſe mariages, whiche ye here meue,
Sens this tale conteinth the counſayle I can geue,
I would ſée your eares attend with your tong,
For aduyſe in bothe theſe weddyngs olde and yong.
In whiche heryng, time ſéene when and what to talke,
When your tonge tickleth, at wyll let it walke.
And in theſe brydales, to the reaſons of ours,
Marke mine experience in this caſe of yours.

The

The ſeuenth chapiter.

VVithin few yeres paſt, from London no far way
   Where I and my wife, with our poore houſhold lay.
Two yong men were abydyng whom to diſcriue.
Were I, in portraiyng perſons dead or aliue,
As cunnyng and as quicke, to touche them at full,
As in that feate I am ignorant and dull,
Neuer could I paynte their pictures to allow,
More liuely, than to paint the pycture of yow.
And as your thrée perſons ſhew one ſimilitewd,
So ſhew you thrée one, in all thingis to be vewd,
Likewyſe a wydowe and a mayde there did dwell,
A lyke lyke the wydow and mayde ye of tell.
The fréendis of theim foure in euery degrée,
Standyng in ſtate as the fréendis of you thrée.
Thoſe two men, eche other ſo haſted or taried,
That thoſe two women on one daie they maried.
Into two houſes, which next my houſe did ſtand,
The one on the right, thother on the lefte hand.
Both bridegromes bad me, I could do none other,
But dine with the tone, and ſup with the tother.
He that wedded this widow riche and olde,
And alſo ſhe, fauourd me ſo, that they wolde
Make me dyne or ſup ones or twyſe in a wéeke.
This poore yonge man and his make beyng to féeke
As oft, where they might eate or drinke, I them bad,
Were I at home, to ſuche pittaunce as I had.
Whiche common conference ſuche confidence wrought,
In them to me, that déede, woorde, ne welny thought
Chaunced among them, what euer it weare,
But one of the foure, brought it ſtreight to mine eare.
Wherby betwene theſe twayne, and their two wyues,
Bothe for welth and wo, I knew all their four liues.

B iij   And

And ſens the matter is muche intricate,
Betwene ſyde and ſyde, I ſhall here ſeperate
All matters on both ſydes, and than ſequeſtrate
Thone ſyde, while thother be full reherſt, in rate,
As for your vnderſtandyng maie beſt ſtande.
And this yonge poore couple ſhall come fyrſt in hande.
Who, the day of weddyng and after, a whyle,
Could not looke eche on other, but they muſt ſmyle.
As a whelpe for wantonnes in and out whipps,
So playde theſe twayne, as mery as thrée chipps.
Ye there was God (quoth he) whan all is doone.
Abyde (quoth I) it was yet but hony moone.
The blacke oxe had not trode on his nor hir foote.
But er this braunche of blis could reach any roote,
The flowers ſo faded, that in fiftene wéekes,
A man might eſpie the chaunge in the chéekes
Both of this poore wretch, and his wife this poore wenche,
Their faces told toies, that Totnam was tournd frenche.
And all their light laughyng turnd and tranſlated
Into ſad ſighyng, all mirth was amated.
And one mornyng tymely he tooke in hande,
To make to my houſe, a fléeueles errande.
Haukyng vpon me, his minde herein to breake,
Whiche I woulde not ſée, tyll he began to ſpeake,
Praiyng me to here him. And I ſaide, I woulde.
Wherwith this that foloweth foorthwith he tolde.

The. viii. chapiter.

I Am nowe driuen (quoth he) for eaſe of my harte,
To you, to vtter parte of mine inward ſmarte.
And the matter concerneth my wyfe and mée,
Whoſe fathers and mothers long ſens dead bée.
But vncles, with auntes and coſins, haue wée
Dyuers riche on bothe ſydes, ſo that we did ſée,

If

14

If we had wedded, eche, where eche kynred would,
Neither of vs had lackt, either ſiluer or gold.
But neuer coulde ſuite, on either ſyde obtayne
One peny, to the one weddyng of vs twayne.
And ſens our one mariyng or marryng daie,
Where any of them ſée vs, they ſhrinke awaie,
Solemnly ſwearyng, ſuche as maie geue ought,
While they and we liue, of them we get right nought.
Nor nought haue we, nor no waie ought can we get,
Sauyng by borowyng, tyll we be in det
So far, that no man any more will vs lende.
Wherby, for lacke we bothe be at our wittis ende.
Wherof no wonder, ſens the ende of our good,
And beginnyng of our charge, together ſtood.
But wit is neuer good tyll it be bought.
Howbeit when bought wits to beſt price bée brought,
Yet is one good forewit woorth two after wits.
This paith me home lo, and full mo foly hits.
For had I lookt afore, with indifferent eye,
Though haſte had made me thurſt neuer ſo drye :
Yet to drowne this drought, this muſt I néedes thynke,
As I woulde néedes brewe, ſo muſt I néedes drynke.
The drynke of my bride cup I ſhould haue forborne,
Tyll temperance had tempred the taſte beforne.
I ſée nowe, and ſhall ſée while I am aliue,
Who wedth or he be wiſe ſhall die or he thriue.
I ſinge nowe in this facte, *factus eſt repente,*
Nowe mine eies be open I do repent me.
He that will ſell lawne before he can folde it.
He ſhall repent him before he haue ſolde it.
Som bargains déere bought, good cheape wold be ſold,
No man loueth his fetters, be they made of gold.
Were I looſe from the louely lynkes of my chayne,
I would not daunce in ſuch fayre fetters agayne.

In

15

In houſe to kepe houſholde, whan folks wyll néedis wed,
Mo thyngs belong, than foure bare legs in a bed.
I reckened my weddyng a ſuger ſwéete ſpyce,
But reckners without their hoſt muſt recken twyce.
And although it were ſwéete for a wéeke or twayne,
Swéete meate will haue ſowre ſawce, I ſée now playne.
Continuall penurie, whiche I muſte take
Telth me, better eye out then alwaie ake.
Boldly and blindly I ventred on this,
How be it, who ſo bolde as blynde Bayard is?
And herein to blame any man, then ſhould I raue.
For I did it my ſelfe: and ſelfe do, ſelfe haue.
But a daie after the fayre, comth this remors,
For reliefe: for though it be a good hors
That neuer ſtumbleth, what praiſe can that auouche
To iades that breake their necks at fyrſt trip or touche.
And before this my fyrſt foyle or breakneck fall,
Subtilly lyke a ſhéepe thought I, I ſhall
Cut my cote after my cloth. When I haue her.
But now I can ſmell, nothyng hath no ſauer.
I am taught to know, in more haſt than good ſpéede,
How *Judicare* came into the Créede.
My carefull wife in one corner wéepeth in care,
And I in an other the purs is thréede bare.
This corner of our care (quoth he) I you tell.
To craue therin your comfortable counſell.

The, ix. chapiter.

I Am ſory (quoth I) of your pouertée,
And more ſorie, that I can not ſuccour yée,
If ye ſtur your néede myne almes to ſtur,
Then of trouth ye beg at a wrong mans dur.
There is nothyng more vayne, as your ſelfe tell can,
Than to beg a bréeche of a bare arſt man.

I

I come to beg nothyng of you (quoth he)
Saue your aduyſe, whiche maie my beſt waie be,
How to wyn preſent ſalue for this preſent ſore.
I am lyke thyll ſurgeon (ſayd I) without ſtore
Of good plaiſters. Howbeit ſuche as they are,
Ye ſhall haue the beſt I haue. But fyrſt declare,
Where your and your wyues riche kynſfolke do dwel.
Enuyronned about vs (quoth he) which ſhewth well,
The nere to the churche, the ferther from God.
Moſt parte of them dwell within a thouſand rod.
And yet ſhall we catche a hare with a taber,
As ſoone as catche ought of them, and rather.
Ye plaie coleprophet (quoth I) who takth in hande,
To knowe his anſwere before he do his errande.
What ſhould I to them (quoth he) flyng or flyt.
An vnbydden geaſt knoweth not where to ſyt.
I am caſt at carts ars, ſome folke in lacke
Can not preaſe, A broken fléeue holdth tharme backe.
And ſhame holdth me backe, beyng thus forſaken.
Tuſhe man (quoth I) ſhame is as it is taken.
And ſhame take him that ſhame thinkth ye thinke none.
Unminded, vnmoned, go make your mone.
Tyll meate fall in your mouth, will ye ly in bed,
Or ſit ſtyll? nay, he that gapeth till he be fed,
Maie fortune to faſt and famiſhe for honger.
Set forward, ye ſhall neuer labour yonger.
Well (quoth he) if I ſhall nedes this viage make,
With as good will as a beare goth to the ſtake,
I will ſtreight weie anker, and hoyſe vp ſayle.
And thytherward hye me in haſte lyke a ſnayle.
And home agayne hytherward quicke as a bée.
Nowe for good lucke, caſte an olde ſhoe after mée.
And firſt to mine vncle, brother to my father,
By ſuite, I will aſſaie to win some ſauer.

C

Who

Who brought me vp, and tyll my weddyng was don
Loued me, not as his nephew, but as his fon.
And his heire had I béene, had not this chaunced,
Of lands and goodes, which fhould me much auaunced.
Trudge (quoth I) to him, and on your marybones,
Crouche to the grounde, and not fo ofte as ones
Speake any one woord him to contrary.
I can not tell that (quoth he) by Seint Mary.
One yll woord axeth an other, as folkis fpeake.
Well (quoth I) better is to boow then breake.
It hurteth not the tounge to geue fayre wurdis.
The rough net is not the beft catcher of burdis.
Sens ye can nought wyn, if ye can not pleafe,
Beft is to fuffre: For of fuffrance comth eafe.
Caufe caufeth (quoth he) and as caufe caufeth mée,
So will I doo. And with this away went hée.
Yet whether his wyfe fhould go with him or no,
He sent hir to me to know er he would go.
Wherto I fayde, I thought beft he went alone.
And you (quoth I) to go ftreight as he is gone,
Among your kynsfolke likewyfe, if they dwell ny.
Yes (quoth fhe) all round about euen here by.
Namely an aunte, my mothers fyfter. who well
(Sens my mother died) brought me vp from the fhell.
And much would haue geuen me, had my weddyng growne
Vpon hir fansy, as it grew vpon mine owne.
And in likewyfe myne vncle hir hufband, was
A father to me. Well (quoth I) let pas:
And if your hufbande will his affent graunt,
Go, he to his vncle, and you to your aunt.
Yes this affent he graunteth before (quoth fhe)
For he er this thought this the beft way to be.
But of thefe two thinges he woulde determine none
Without ayde. For two heddis are better then one.

With

With this we departed, ſhe to hir huſbande,
And I to diner to them on thother hande.

The. *x. chapiter.*

VVhan diner was doone, I came home agayne,
   To attende on the retourne of theſe twayne.
And er thrée howres to ende were fully tryde,
Home came ſhe fyrſt, welcome (quoth I) and well hyde.
Ye a ſhort horſe is ſoone corryd (quoth ſhée)
But the weaker hath the wurs we all daie ſée.
After our laſt partyng, my huſbande and I
Departed, eche to place agréed formerly.
Myne vncle and aunte on me dyd loure and glome.
Bothe bad me god spéede, but none bad me welcome.
Their folkis glomd on me to, by which it apéereth.
The yonge cocke croweth, as he the olde héereth.
At dyner they were, and made (for maners ſake)
A kynſwoman of ours me to table take.
A falſe flattryng ſylth, and if that be good,
None better to beare two faces in one hood.
She ſpeaketh as ſhe would créepe into your boſome.
And when the meale mouth hath woon the bottome
Of your ſtomake, than will the pickthanke it tell
To your moſt enmies, you to bye and ſell.
To tell tales out of ſchoole, that is hir great luſt.
Looke what ſhe knowth, blab it wiſt, and out it muſt.
There is no mo ſuch titifyls in Englands ground,
To holde with the hare, and run with the hound.
Fyre in the tone hande, and water in the tother,
The makebate beareth betwéene brother and brother.
She can wynke on the yew, and wery the lam.
She maketh earneſt matters of euery flymflam.
She muſt haue an ore in euery mans barge.
And no man may chat ought in ought of hir charge.

Coll vnder canſtyk, ſhe can plaie on bothe handis,
Diſſimulacion well ſhe vnderſtandis.
She is loſt with an apple, and woon with a nut.
Her tong is no edge toole, but yet it will cut.
Her chéekes are purple ruddie lyke a horſe plumme.
And the bygge parte of hir bodie is hir bumme.
But little titte all tayle, I haue heard er this,
As high as twoo horſe loues hir perſon is.
For priuie nyps or caſts ouertwart the ſhyns,
He ſhall leſe the maiſtrie that with hir begyns.
She is, to turne loue to hate, or ioye to gréefe
A paterne, as méete as a rope for a théefe.
Her promiſe of fréendſhip, for any auayle,
Is as ſure to holde as an ele by the tayle.
She is nother fyſhe nor fleſhe, nor good red hearyng.
She is a ryngleader there, And I fearyng
She would ſpit her venym, thought it not euyll
To ſette vp a candle before the deuyll.
I clawd hir by the backe in waie of a charme,
To do me, not the more good, but the leſſe harme.
Praiyng hir in hir eare, on my ſyde to holde,
She therto ſwearyng by her falſe faith, ſhe wolde.
Streight after diner myne aunte had no choice,
But other burſt, or burſt out in pilats voice.
Ye huſwife, what wynde blowth ye hyther thus right ?
Ye might haue knokt er ye came in, leaue is light.
Better vnborne than vntought, I haue heard ſaie,
But ye be better fed then taught farre awaie.
Not very fat fed, ſaid this ſlebergebet,
But néede hath no lawe, néede maketh hir hither iet.
She comth néece Ales (quoth ſhe) for that is hir name,
More for néede, than for kyndnes, peyne of ſhame.
Howbeit ſhe can not lacke, for he ſyndth that féekes,
Louers liue by loue, ye as larkes liue by léekes

Saied

Saied this Ales, muche more then halfe in mockage.
Tuſhe (quoth mine aunte) theſe louers in dotage
Thinke the ground beare them not, but wed of corage
They muſt in all haſte, though a leafe of borage
Might by all the ſubſtance that they can ſell.
Well aunt (quoth Ales) all is well that endes well.
Ye Ales, of a good begynnyng comth a good end.
Not ſo good to borowe, as be able to lend.
Naie in déede aunte (quoth ſhe) it is ſure ſo,
She muſt nedes grant, ſhe hath wrought hir owne wo.
She thought Ales, ſhe had féene far in a milſtone,
Whan ſhe gat a huſbande, and namely ſuche one,
As they by weddyng could not onely nought wyn,
But loſe bothe liuyng and loue of all their kyn.
Good aunt (quoth I) humblie I beſeche yée,
My treſpas doone to you forgeue it mée.
I know and knowlage, I haue wrought mine owne peyn,
But thingis paſt my handis, I can not call agein.
True (quoth Ales) thinges doone can not be vndoone,
Be they done in due tyme, to late, or to ſoone,
But better late then neuer to repent this,
To late (quoth mine aunt) this repentance ſhewd is,
Whan the ſtéede is ſtolne ſhut the ſtable durre.
I toke hir for a roſe, but ſhe bréedth a burre.
She comth to ſticke to me nowe in hir lacke.
Rather to rent of my clothes fro my backe,
Than to do me one farthyng woorth of good.
I ſée daie at this little hole. For this bood
Shewth what fruite will folow. In good faith I ſaide,
In waie of peticion I ſue for your ayde.
A well (quoth ſhe) now I well vnderſtand
The walkyng ſtaffe hath caught warmth in your hand.
A cleane fingred huſwyfe, and an ydell, folke ſaie,
And wyll be lyme fyngerd I feare by my fay.

C iij   It

It is as tender as a parſons lemman.
Nought can ſhe dooe, and what can ſhe haue than?
As ſober as ſhe ſeemth, fewe daies come about
But ſhe will onece waſſhe hir face in an ale clout.
And than betwene hir and the reſt of the rout,
I proud, and thou proud, who ſhall beare thaſhes out.
She maie not beare a fether, but ſhe muſt breath,
She maketh ſo much of hir peynted ſheath.
She thinkth her farthyng good ſyluer I tell you,
But for a farthyng who euer did ſell you,
Myght boſt you to be better ſolde then bought.
And yet though ſhe be woorth nought, nor haue nought,
Her gowne is gaier and better then mine.
At hir gaie gowne (quoth Ales) ye maie repine.
Howe be it as we maie we loue to go gaie all.
Well well (quoth mine aunte) pryde wyll haue a fall.
For pryde goeth before, and ſhame cometh after.
Sure (ſaide Ales) in maner of mockyng laughter,
There is nothing in this worlde that agréeth wurs,
Then dooeth a Ladies hert and a beggers purs.
But pryde ſhe ſhewth none, hir looke reaſon alouth,
She lookth as butter wolde not melte in hir mouth.
Well the ſtill ſowe eats vp all the draffe Ales.
All is not golde that gliſters by tolde tales.
In youth ſhe was towarde and without euill.
But ſoone rype ſoone rotten, yong ſeynt olde deuill.
How be it lo god ſendth the ſhrewd coow ſhort hornes.
While ſhe was in this houſe ſhe ſat vpon thornes.
Eche one daie was thrée, tyll lybertée was borow,
For one monthis ioie to bryng hir hole liues ſorow.
It were pitie (quoth Ales) but ſhe ſhould do well.
For beautie and ſtature ſhe beareth the bell.
Ill wéede growth faſt Ales: wherby the corne is lorne.
For ſurely the wéede ouergroweth the corne.

Ye

Ye praiſe the wyne, before ye taſt of the grape.
But ſhe can no more harme than can a ſhe ape.
It is a good body, hir propertie préeues.
She lacketh but euen a new payre of ſléeues.
If I maie (as they say) tell trouth without ſyn.
Of trouth ſhe is a wolfe in a lambes ſkyn.
Her herte is full hie, whan her eye is full low.
A geſt as good loſt as founde, for all this ſhow.
But many a good coowe hath an euill caulfe.
I ſpeake this doughter in thy mothers behalfe.
My ſiſter (God reſt hir ſoule) whom though I boſt,
Was cald the floure of honeſtée in this coſt.
Aunt (quoth I) I take for father and mother
Myne vncle and you aboue all other.
When we wold, ye wold not be our childe (quoth ſhée)
Wherfore now whan ye wold, now will not wée.
Sens thou wouldſt néedes caſt awaie thy ſelfe thus,
Thou ſhalte ſure ſinke in thine own ſyn for vs.
Aunt (quoth I) after a dotyng or dronken déede,
Let ſubmiſſion obteine ſome mercie or méede.
He that kylth a man, whan he is dronke (quoth ſhe)
Shalbe hangd when he is ſobre. And he
Whom in itching no ſcratchyng will forbere,
He muſt beare the ſmartyng that ſhall folow there.
And thou beyng borne very nigh of my ſtocke,
Though ny be my kyrtell, yet nere is my ſmocke.
I haue one of mine owne whom I muſt looke to.
Ye aunt (quoth Ales) that thinge muſte ye néedes do.
Nature compelth you to ſet your owne fyrſt vp.
For I haue heard ſaie, it is a déere colup
That is cut out of thowne fleſhe. But yet aunte,
So ſmall maie hir requeſt be, that ye maie graunte
To ſatiſſie the ſame, whiche maie do her good,
And you no harme in thauanſyng your owne blood.

And

23

And coſin (quoth ſhe to me) what ye would craue,
Declare, that our aunt may know what ye would haue.
Nay (quoth I) be they wynners or looſers,
Folke ſaie alwaie, beggers ſhould be no chooſers.
With thankes I ſhall take what euer mine aunte pleaſe.
Where nothyng is, a little thyng dooth eaſe,
Hunger makth hard beanes ſwéete. where ſaddles lacke
Better ride on a pad, than on the horſe bare backe.
And by this prouerbe apéerth this o thyng,
That alwaie ſomwhat is better then nothyng.
Hold faſt whan ye haue it (quoth ſhe) by my lyfe.
The boy thy huſbande, and thou the gyrle his wyfe,
Shall not conſume that I haue laboured fore.
Thou art yong inough, and I can woorke no more.
Kyt calot my cooſyn ſawe this thus far on,
And in mine auntis eare ſhe whiſpreth anon
Roundly theſe woordes, to make this matter whole.
Aunt, leat them that be a colde blowe at the cole.
They ſhall for me Ales (quoth ſhe) by gods blyſt.
She and I haue ſhaken handes. farewell vnkyſt.
And thus with a becke as good as a dieu gard,
She ſlang fro me, and I from hir hitherward.
Beggyng of hir booteth not the woorth of a beane.
Littell knoweth the fat ſow, what the leane dooth meane.
Forſooth (quoth I) ye haue beſtyrd ye well.
But where was your vncle whyle all this fray fell?
A ſléepe by (quoth ſhe) routyng lyke a hog.
And it is euyll wakyng of a ſléepyng dog.
The bytche and hir whelpe might haue béene a ſléepe to,
For ought they in wakyng to me would do.
Fare ye well (quoth ſhe) I will nowe home ſtreite,
And at my huſbandis handis for better newes weite.

The

24

The. xi. chapiter.

H E came home to me the next daie before noone.
What tydingis now (quoth I) how haue ye doone?
Vpon our departyng (quoth he) yeſterdaie
Toward mine vncles, ſomwhat more than mydway,
I ouertooke a man, a ſeruaunt of his,
And a fréend of myne. Who geſſed ſtreight with this
What mine errand was, offryng in the ſame,
To do his beſt for me, and ſo in gods name,
Thyther we went, no body beyng within,
But myne vncle, myne aunte, and one of our kyn.
A mad knaue, as it were a raylyng geſter,
Not a more gagglyng gander henſe to Cheſter.
At ſight of me he aſked, who haue we there?
I haue féene this gentleman, if I wiſt where.
Howe be it lo, ſeldome féene, ſoone forgotten.
He was (as he will be) ſomwhat cupſhotten.
Sixe daies in the wéeke beſide the market daie.
Malt is aboue wheate with him. market men ſaie.
But for as muche as I ſawe the ſame taunt
Contented well mine vncle and mine aunt.
And that I cam to fall in, and not to fall out,
I forbare: or els his dronken red ſnout,
I would haue made as oft chaunge from hew to hew,
As dooth the cocks of Inde. For this is trew,
It is a ſmall hop on my thombe. And Chriſt wot,
It is wood at a woorde. little potte ſoone whot.
Nowe mery as a cricket, and by and by,
Angry as a waſpe, though in both no cauſe why.
But he was at home there, he might ſpeake his will.
Euery cocke is proude on his owne dunghill.
I ſhall be euen with him herein whan I can.
But he hauyng done, thus myne vncle began.

D   Ye

Ye marchant, what attempth you, to attempt vs,
To come on vs before the meſſenger thus?
Roming in an out, I here tell how ye toſſe.
But ſonne, the rollyng ſtone neuer gatherth moſſe.
Lyke a pyckpurs pilgrim, ye prie and ye proule
At rouers, to rob Peter and paie Poule.
Iwys I know, or any more be tolde,
That draffe is your errand, but drinke ye wolde.
Vncle (quoth I) of the cauſe, for whiche I com,
I pray you paciently here the hole ſom.
In fayth (quoth he) without any more ſummyng,
I know to beg of me is thy commyng,
Forſoth (quoth his man) it is ſo in déede.
And I dare boldly boſte, if ye knewe his néede,
Ye wolde of pittie yet ſet him in ſome ſtey.
Sonne, better be enuied than pitied, folke ſey.
And for his cauſe of pitée (had he had grace)
He might this daie haue béene cleere out of the caſe.
But now he hath well fyſht and caught a frog.
Where nought is to wed with, wiſe men flée the clog.
Where I (quoth I) did not as ye wyld or bad,
That repent I oft, and as oft wiſhe I had.
Sonne (quoth he) as I haue herd of myne olders,
Wiſhers and wolders be no good houſeholders.
This prouerbe for a leſſon, with ſuch other.
Not lyke (as who ſaieth) the ſonne of my brother,
But lyke mine owne ſonne, I ofte before tolde the,
To caſt hir quite of, but it woulde not holde the.
Whan I wyld the any other where to go,
Tuſhe, there was no mo maydes but malkyn tho.
Ye had béen loſt to lacke your luſt, whan ye lyſt,
By two myles trudgeyng twyſe a wéeke to be kyſt.
I would ye had kyſt, well I will no more ſturre.
It is good to haue a hatche before the durre.

But

26

But who will in tyme preſent pleaſure refrayne,
Shall in time to come, the more pleaſure obtayne.
Folowe pleaſure, and then will pleaſure flée.
Flée pleaſure, and pleaſure will folowe thée,
And howe is my ſaiyng come to paſſe nowe?
How oft did I prophecie this betwéene you
And your giniſinée nycebecetur?
Whan ſwéete ſuger ſhould tourne to ſoure ſalte petur,
Wherby ye ſhould in ſeyng that ye neuer ſawe,
Thynke that you neuer thought. your ſelfe a dawe.
But that tyme ye thought me a dawe. ſo that I
Dyd no good in all my woordes then, ſaue onely
Approued this prouerbe playne and true mater,
A man maie well bring a horſe to the water,
But he can not make him drinke without he will.
Colts (quoth his man) may proue well with tatches yll.
For of a ragged colte there comth a good horſe.
If he be good now of his ill paſt no force.
Well, he that hangth him ſelfe a ſondaie (ſaid hée)
Shall hang ſtill vncut downe a mondaie for mée.
I haue hangd vp my hatchet, God ſpéede him well.
A wonder thing what thingis theſe olde thinges tell.
Cat after kynde good mouſe hunt. And alſo
Men ſaie, kinde will créepe where it maie not go.
Commenly all thyng ſhewth fro whens it camme.
The litter is lyke to the ſyre and the damme.
How can the fole amble, if the hors and mare trot?
Theſe ſentenſes are aſſigned vnto thy lot,
By condicions of thy father and mother,
My ſyſter in lawe, and mine owne ſaid brother.
Thou foloweſt their ſteppes as right as a lyne.
For when prouander prickt them a little tyne,
They did as thy wife and thou did, both dote
Eche one on other, and beyng not woorth a grote,

D ij

They

27

They went (witleſſe) to wedding. Wherby at laſt
They both went a beggyng. And euen the lyke caſt
Haſt thou. thou wilt beg or ſteale, er thou dye.
Take héede fréende I haue ſéene as far come as nye.
If ye féeke to fynde thynges, er they be loſt,
Ye ſhall fynde one daie you come to your coſt.
This doo I but repete, for this I tolde thée,
And more I ſaie: but I could not then holde thée.
Nor will not holde the now: nor ſuche foly féele,
To ſet at my hert that thou ſetteſt at thy héele.
And as of my good, er I one grote géeue,
I wyll ſée how my wyfe, and my ſelfe maie léeue.
Thou goeſt a glenyng er the cart haue caried.
But er thou gleine ought, ſens thou woldſt be maried
Shall I make the laugh now, and my ſelfe wéepe then?
Naie good childe, better children wéepe then olde men.
Men ſhould not preſe much, to ſpend much vpon fooles.
Fiſhe is caſte awaie that is caſt in drie pooles.
To flée charge, and fynde eaſe, ye wold now héere ofte.
It is eaſy to cry vle at other mens coſte.
But a bow long bent, at length muſt ware weake.
Long bent I toward you, but that bent I will breake.
Fare well and féede full, that loue ye well to do.
But you luſt not to doo, that longeth therto.
The cat would eate fyſhe, and would not wet her féete.
They muſt hunger in froſt, that will not woorke in héete.
And he that will thriue, muſt aſke leaue of his wife.
But your wife will geue none, by your and hir life.
It is harde to wiue and thryue bothe in a yere.
Thus by thy wyuyng, thryuyng dooth ſo appere,
That thou art paſt thrift before thryft begyn.
But lo, wyll wyll haue wyll, though will wo wyn,
Will is a good ſonne, and will is a ſhrewde boy.
And wilfull ſhrewde will hath wrought thée this toy.

A

A gentle white ſpurre, and at néede a ſure ſpeare.
He ſtandth now as he had a flea in his eare.
How be it for any great courteſie he doth make,
It féemth the gentill man hath eaten a ſtake.
He beareth a dagger in his ſleue, truſt mée,
To kyll all that he méeteth prouder then hée.
He will perke, I here ſay he muſt haue the benche.
Iacke would be a gentleman if he could ſpeake frenche.
He thinkth his féete be, where his head ſhall neuer come.
He would fayne flée, but he wanteth fethers, ſome.
Sir (quoth his man) he will no faute defende
But harde is for any man all fautes to mende.
He is liueles, that is fautles, olde folkes thought.
He hath (quoth he) but one faute, he is nought.
Well (quoth his man) the beſt cart maie ouerthrowe.
Cartis well driuen (quoth he) go longe vpright thowe.
But for my rewarde, let him be no longer tarier.
I will ſend it him, by Iohn Longe the carier.
O helpe him ſir (ſaide he) ſens ye eaſily maie.
Shamfull crauyng (quoth he) muſt haue ſhamefull naie.
Ye maie ſyr (quoth he) mend thrée naies with one yée.
Two falſe knaues néede no broker, men ſay (ſaid hée)
Some ſaie alſo it is mery when knaues méete.
But the mo knaues the woorſe company to gréete.
The one knaue now croucheth, while thother crauith.
But to ſhew what ſhalbe his releuauith.
Either after my death if my will be kept,
Or duryng my lyfe : had I this hall hept
With golde, he maie his parte on good fridaie eate,
And faſt neuer the wurs, for ought he ſhall geate.
Theſe former leſſons conde, take foorth this, ſonne.
Tell thy cardes, and than tell me what thou haſt wonne.
Now here is the doore, and there is the wey,
And ſo (quoth he) farewell gentill Geffrey.

               D iij   Thus

Thus parted I from him, beyng muche diſmaide,
Whiche his man ſawe, and (to comfort me) ſaied.
What man, plucke vp your hert, be of good chéere.
After cloudes blacke, we ſhall haue weather cléere.
What ſhould your face thus agayne the woll be ſhorne
For one fall? What man all this winde ſhakis no corne.
Let this winde ouerblow. a tyme I will ſpy,
To take wynde and tyde with me, and ſpede therby.
I thanke you (quoth I) but great boſt and ſmall roſte,
Maketh vnſauery mouthes, where ever men ofte.
And this boſte veraie vnſauorly ſerueth.
For while the graſſe groweth the horſe ſterueth.
Better one byrde in hande than ten in the wood.
Rome was not built in one daie (quoth he) and yet ſtood.
Till it was finiſht, as ſome ſay, full faire.
Your hert is in your hoſe all in diſpaire.
But as euery man ſaith, a dog hath a daie.
Should you a man, diſpaire than any daie? naie.
Ye haue many ſtryngis to the bowe, for ye know.
Though I, hauyng the bent of your vncles bow,
Can no way bryng your bolte in the but to ſtand,
Yet haue ye other markis to roue at hand.
The kays hang not all by one mans gyrdell man.
Though nought wilbe woon here, I ſay, yet ye can
Taſte other kinſmen, of whom ye may geat,
Here ſome and there ſome, many ſmall make a great.
For come lyght winnynges with bleſſings or curſes,
Euermore light gaynes make heauy purſes.
Children learne to créepe er they can learne to go.
And little and little, ye muſt learne euen ſo.
Throw no gyft agayne at the geuers head,
For better is halfe a lofe than no bread.
I maie beg my bread (quoth I) for my kyn all
That dwelth ny. Well, yet (quoth he) and the woorſt fall,

Ye

Ye maie to your kinſman, hens nine or ten mile.
Riche without charge, whom ye ſaw not of long while.
That benchwhiſtler (quoth I) is a pinchpeny,
As free of gyft, as a poore man of his eie.
I ſhall geat a fart of a dead man as ſoone
As a farthyng of him, his dole is ſoone doone.
He is ſo hy in thinſtep, and ſo ſtreight laſte,
That pryde and couetyſe withdrawth all repaſte,
Ye know what he hath béene (quoth he) but iwis,
Abſence ſaith plainly, ye know not what he is.
Men know (quoth I) I haue herd now and then,
How the market goth by the market men.
Further it is ſaide, who that ſaiyng wayth,
It muſt néedes be true, that euery man ſayth.
Men ſay alſo, children and fooles can not ly.
And both man and child ſaieth, he is a heinſby.
And my ſelfe knowth him, I dare boldly brag,
Euen as well as the begger knowth his bag.
And I knew him, not woorth a grey grote.
He was at an ebbe, though he be now a flote,
Poore as the pooreſt. And now nought he ſetteth
By poore folke, For the paryſhe prieſt forgetteth
That euer he hath bene holy water clarke.
By ought I can now here, or euer could marke.
Of no man hath he pitie or compaſſion.
Well (quoth he) euery man after his faſſion.
He maie yet pitie you, for ought doth appéere,
It hapth in one houre, that hapth not in. vii. yere.
Forſpeake not your fortune, nor hide not your néede.
Nought venter nought haue. ſpare to ſpeake ſpare to ſpéede.
Vnknowne vnkyſt. it is loſte that is vnsought.
As good féeke nought (quoth I) as feeke and finde nought.
It is (quoth he) yll fyſhyng before the net.
But though we get little, dere bought and far fet.

                                                    Are

31

Are deinties for Ladies. Go we both twoo,
I haue for my maiſter thereby to doo,
I maie breake a diſhe there. and ſure I ſhall
Set all at ſixe and ſeuen, to win ſome windfall.
And I will hang the bell about the cats necke.
For I will firſt breake, and ieobard the firſt checke.
And for to wyn this praie, though the coſt be mine,
Leat vs preſent him with a bottle of wyne.
What ſhould we (quoth I) greaſe the fat ſow in thars,
We maie doo much ill, er we doo much wars.
It is, to geue him, as muche almes or néede
As caſt water in tems, or as good a déede,
As it is to helpe a dogge ouer a ſtyle.
Than go we (quoth he) we leſe tyme all this while.
To folow his fancy, we went together.
And toward night yeſternight when we came thyther,
She was within, but he was yet abrode.
And ſtreight as ſhe ſawe me, ſhe ſwelde lyke a tode.
Pattryng the diuels Pater noſter to hir ſelfe,
God neuer made a more crabbed elfe.
She bad him welcome, but the wurs for mée.
This knaue comth a beggyng, by me thought ſhée.
I ſmelde hir out, and had hir ſtreight in the wynde.
She maie abide no beggers of any kynde.
They be both gréedy guts all geuen to get.
They care not how: all is fiſhe that comth to net.
They know no ende of their good: nor beginnyng
Of any goodneſſe. ſuche is wretched winnyng.
Hunger droppeth euen out of bothe their noſes.
She goth with broken ſhone and torne hoſes
But who is wurs ſhod, than the ſhoemakers wyfe,
With ſhops full of newe ſhoes all hir lyfe?
Or who will doo leſſe, then they that may do moſte?
And namely of hir I can no waie make boſte.

She

She is one of them, to whom God bad who.
She will all haue, and will right nought forgo.
She will not part with the paryng of hir nayles,
She toyleth continually for auayles.
Whiche life ſhe hath ſo long now kept in vre.
That for no life ſhe wolde make chaunge, be ſure.
But this leſſon lernde I, er I was yeres ſeuen.
They that be in hell, wene there is none other heuen.
She is nothyng fayre, but ſhe is yll fauourd.
And no more vnclenly, than vnſwéete ſauourd.
But hakney men ſaie, at mangy hackneis hyer,
A ſcald hors is good inough for a ſcabde ſquyer.
He is a knuckylbonyard veraie méete
To matche a minion nother fayre nor ſwéete.
He winkth with the tone eie, and lokth with the tother
I will not truſt him though he were my brother.
He hath a poyſon wyt, and all his delyte,
To geue tauntes and checkes of moſt ſpitefull ſpyte.
In that houſe commonly ſuch is the caſt,
A man ſhall as ſoone breake his necke as his faſt.
And yet nowe ſuche a gyd did hir head take,
That more for my mates then for maners ſake.
We had bread and drinke, and a chéeſe very greate.
But the greatteſt crabs be not all the beſt meate.
For hir crabbed chéeſe, with all the greatneſſe,
Myght well abide the fineneſſe, or ſweatneſſe,
Anon he cam in. And when he vs ſawe,
To my companion kindlie he did drawe.
And a well fauourd welcome to him he yéelds.
Byddyng me welcome ſtrangly ouer the féelds.
With theſe woordes, Ah yong man I know your matter,
By my faith you come to looke in my water.
And for my comfort to your conſolacion,
Ye would, by my purs, geue me a purgacion.

                    E   But

But I am laxatiue inough there otherwiſe.
This (quoth this yonge man) contrary doth ryſe.
For he is purs ſicke, and lackth a phiſicion,
And hopeth vpon you in ſome condicion.
Not by purgacion, but by reſtoratiue.
To ſtrength his weakeneſſe to kéepe him aliue.
I can not (quoth he) for though it be my lot
To haue ſpeculacion, yet I practyſe not.
I ſée muche, but I ſay little, and doo leſſe,
In this kinde of phiſicke. and what would ye geſſe,
Shall I conſume my ſelfe, to reſtore him now ?
Nay, backare (quoth mortimer to his ſow)
He can before this tyme, no tyme aſſine,
In whiche he hath laied downe one peny by myne,
That euer might either make me bite or ſup.
And byr lady fréed, nought lay downe, nought take vp.
Ka me, ka the, one good tourne aſkth an other.
Nought woon by the tone, nought won by the tother.
To put me to coſte, thou camſt halfe a ſcore myles,
Out of thine owne neſt, to féeke me in theſe out yles.
Where thou wilt not ſtep ouer a ſtraw, I thynke,
To wyn me the woorth of one draught of drynke.
No more than I haue wonne of all thy hole ſtocke.
I haue bene common Iacke to all that hole flocke.
Whan ought was to doo, I was common hackney,
Folke call on the horſe that will cary alwey.
But euermore the common horſe is woorſt ſhod.
Deſert and rewarde be oft tymes thynges far od.
At end I might put my winnyng in mine eye,
And ſée neuer the woorſe, for ought I wan them bye.
And now without them, I liue here at ſtaues end.
Where I néed not borowe, nor I will not lend.
It is good to beware by other mens harmes,
But thy takyng of thyne aulter in thine armes.

Teacheth

Teacheth other to beware of their harmes by thyne.
Thou haſt ſtriken the ball, vnder the lyne.
I praie you (quoth I) pitie me a poore man,
With ſomewhat, tyll I maie woorke as I can.
Toward your woorkyng (quoth he) ye make ſuch taſtingis,
As approue you to be none of the haſtingis.
Ye ren to woorke in haſte as nine men helde ye.
But whan ſo euer ye to woorke muſt yeld ye.
If your meete mate and you méete together,
Than ſhall we ſée two men beare a fether.
Recompenſyng former loytryng lyfe looſe,
As dyd the pure penitent that ſtale a gooſe
And ſtack downe a fether. And where olde folke tell,
That euill gotten good neuer proueth well.
Ye wyll truely get, and true gettyng well kéepe
Till time ye be as ryche as a new ſhorne ſhéepe:
Howe be it whan thrift and you fell fyrſt at a fray,
You played the man, for ye made thrift ren away.
So helpe me god, in my poore opinion,
A man might make a plaie of this minion.
And fain no ground, but take tales of his owne fréends,
I ſucke not this out of my owne fingers éends.
And ſens ye were wed, although I nought gaue you,
Yet pray I for you, God and ſaint Luke ſaue you.
And here is all. For what ſhould I further wade?
I was neyther of court nor of counſayle made.
And it is, as I haue lerned in lyſtnyng,
A poore dogge, that is not woorth the whyſtlyng.
A daie er I was wedde, I bad you (quoth I)
Scarbrough warnyng I had (quoth he) wherby,
I kept me thens, to ſerue the accordyng.
And now if this nightes lodgeyng and bordyng.
Maie eaſe the, and ryd me from any more charge,
Then welcome, or els get the ſtreight at large.

E ij   For

35

For of further rewarde, marke how I boſt me,
In caſe as ye ſhall yelde me as ye coſt me,
So ſhall ye coſt me as ye yelde me likewiſe.
Whiche is, a thing of nought rightly to ſurmyſe.
Here with all his wife to make vp my mouthe,
Not onely hir huſbandes tauntyng tale auouthe,
But therto deuiſeth to caſt in my téeth,
Checks and chokyng oyſters. And whan ſhe ſéeth
Her tyme to take vp, to ſhew my fare at beſt,
Ye ſée your fare (ſayd ſhe) ſet your hert at reſt.
Fare ye well (quoth I) how euer I fare now.
And well mote ye fare bothe whan I dyne with yow.
Come, go we hens friend (quoth I to my mate)
And now will I make a croſſe on this gate.
And I (quoth he) croſſe the quyte out of my booke.
Sens thou art croſſe ſaylde, auale vnhappie hooke.
By hooke or crooke nought could I wyn there, men ſay
He that comth euery daie, ſhall haue a cocknaie.
He that comth now and then, ſhall haue a fatte hen.
But I gat not ſo muche in comyng ſéelde when,
As a good hens fether, or a poore egſhell.
As good play for nought as woorke for nought, folke tell.
Well well (quoth he) we be but where we were.
Come what come would, I thought er we came there,
That if the woorſt fell, we could haue but a naie.
There is no harme doone man in all this fraie.
Neither pot broken, nor water ſpylt.
Farewell he (quoth I) I will as ſoone be hylt,
As waite againe for the mooneſhine in the water.
But is not this a prety pyked mater?
To diſdeygne me, who mucke of the worlde hoordth not,
As he dooth, it may ryme but it accordth not.
She ſometh lyke a bore, the beaſt ſhould ſéeme bolde.
For ſhe is as fierce, as a Lyon of Cotſolde.

She

36

She fryeth in hir owne greaſe, but as for my parte,
If ſhe be angry, beſhrew her angry harte.
Fréend (quoth he) he maie ſhewe wiſdome at will,
That with angry herte can holde his tongue ſtyll.
Let pacience growe in your gardein alwaie.
Some looſe or od ende will come man, ſome one daie
From ſome fréende, eyther in lyfe or at death.
Death (quoth I) take we that tyme, to take a breath?
Than graffe we a greene graffe on a rotten roote,
Who waitth for dead men ſhoen, ſhall go long barefoote
Let paſſe (quoth he) and leat vs be trudgeing,
Where ſome noppy ale is, and ſofte ſwéete ludgeing.
Be it (quoth I) but I would very fayne eate.
At breackfaſt and diner I éete little meate.
And two hongry meales make the thyrd a glutten:
We went where we had boylde béefe and bake mutton,
Wherof I fed me as fulle as a tunne.
And a bed were we er the clocke had nine runne.
Early we roſe, in haſt to get awaie,
And to the hoſtler this mornyng by daie
This felow calde. what how felow, thou knaue,
I pray the leat me and my felow haue
A heare of the dog that bote vs laſt night.
And bitten were we both to the braine aright,
We ſawe eche other drunke in the good ale glas,
And ſo did eche one eche other, that there was.
Saue one, but olde men ſay that are ſkyld,
A hard foughten féeld, where no man ſkapth vnkyld.
The recknyng reckned he, néeds would pay the ſhot,
And nedes he muſt ror me, for I had it not.
This doone we ſhoke handes, and parted in fyne,
He into his waie, and I into myne.
But this iourney was quite out of my waie.
Many kynſſolke and few fréends, ſome folke ſaie.

E iij

But

But I fynde many kynſfolke, and fréende not one.
Folke ſay, it hath béene ſaide many yeres ſens gone,
Proue thy fréende er thou haue néede, but in déede
A fréende is neuer knowen tyll a man haue néede.
Before I had néede, my moſt preſent foes
Semed my moſt fréends, but thus the world goes,
Euery man baſteth the fat hog we ſée,
But the leane ſhall burne er he baſted bée.
As ſeyth this ſentence, oft and long ſayd before,
He that hath plentie of goodes ſhall haue more,
He that hath but a little, he ſhall haue leſſe.
He that hath right nought, right nought ſhall poſſeſſe.
Thus hauing right nought, and would ſomwhat obtayne.
With right nought (quoth he) I am retournd againe.

The. xii. chapiter.

SUrely (quoth I) ye haue in this time thus worne,
Made a long harueſt for a little corne.
Howbeit, comforte your ſelfe with this old text,
That telth vs, when bale is hekſt, boote is next.
Though euery man may not ſyt in the chayre.
Yet alwaie the grace of God is woorth a fayre.
Take no thought in no caſe, God is where he was.
But put caſe in pouertée all your life pas.
Yet pouertee and poore degrée, taken well,
Féedth on this, he that neuer climbde, neuer fell.
And ſome caſe at ſome tyme ſhewth préefe ſomwhere,
That riches bringth oft harme, and euer feare.
Where pouertée paſſeth without grudge of gréefe.
What man, the begger maie ſyng before the théefe,
And who can ſyng ſo mery a note,
As maie he, that can not chaunge a grote.
Ye (quoth he) beggers maie ſyng before théeues,
And weepe before true men, lamentyng their greeues.

Some

38

Some ſaie, and I feele hunger perſeth ſtone wall.
Meate nor yet money to bye meate withall,
Haue I not ſo muche as maie hunger defende
Fro my wyfe and me. Well (quoth I) God will ſende
Tyme to prouyde for tyme, right well ye ſhall ſée.
God ſende that prouiſion in tyme (ſaid he.)
And thus ſéemyng welnie wery of his lyfe,
The poore wretch went to his like poore wretched wyfe.
From wantonnes to wretchedneſſe, brought on their knees.
Their hartes full heauy, their heades be full of bees.
And after this a monthe, or ſomwhat leſſe,
Their landlorde came to their houſe to take a ſtreſſe
For rent, to haue kept Bayard in the ſtable.
But that to win, any power was vnable.
For though it be ill plaiyng with ſhort daggers,
Whiche meaneth, that euery wiſe man ſtaggers,
In earneſt or boorde to be buſie or bolde
With his biggers or betters, yet this is tolde.
Where as nothing is, the kynge muſt loſe his right.
And thus, kyng or keyſer muſt haue ſet them quight.
But warnyng to departe thens they neded none.
For er the next daie the birdes were flowne eche one,
To ſéeke ſeruyce. of whiche where the man was ſped,
The wife could not ſpéede, but maugre hir hed,
She muſt ſéeke elswhere. for eyther there or ny,
Seruyce for any ſuite ſhe none could eſpy.
All folke thought them not onely to lyther,
To lynger bothe in one houſe togyther.
But alſo dwellyng ny vnder their wyngs,
Vnder their noſes, they might conuey thinges,
Suche as were neither to heauie nor to whot.
More in a month then they their maiſter got
In a whole yere. Wherto folke further weiyng,
Receiue eche of other in their conueiyng,

                                        Might

39

Might be worſt of all. For this prouerbe préeues,
Where be no receiuers, there be no théeues.
Suche hap here hapt, that common dreade of ſuch gyles
Droue them and kepth them a ſunder many myles.
Thus though loue decrée, departure death to bée,
Yet pouertie parteth felowſhip we ſée.
And doth thoſe two true louers ſo diſſeuer,
That méete ſhall they ſéelde when, or haply neuer.
And thus by loue, without regard of liuyng,
Theſe twayne haue wrought eche others yll chiuyng.
And loue hath ſo loſt them the loue of their fréendis,
That I thinke them loſt, and thus this tale éendis.

The. xiij. chapiter.

AH ſir (ſaid my fréend) when men will néedis mary,
I see now, how wiſdome and haſt maie varie,
Namely where they wed for loue altogether.
I would for no good, but I had come hyther.
Swéete beautie with foure beggery, naie I am gon,
To the welthy wythered wydow, by Sent Iohn.
What yet in all haſte (quoth I) Ye (q̊ hee)
For ſhe hath ſubſtance inough. and ye ſee,
That lacke is the loſſe of theſe two yong fooles.
Know ye not (quoth I) that after wiſe mens ſchooles,
A man ſhould here all partis, er he iudge any?
Why axe ye that (quoth he.) For this (quoth I.
I tolde you, whan I this began that I woulde
Tell you of two couples. and I hauyng told
But of the tone, ye be ſtreight ſtartyng away,
As I of the tother had right nought to ſay.
Or as your ſelfe of them right nought wold here.
Naie not all ſo (quoth he) but ſyns I thynke clere,
There can no way appeere ſo peinfull a lyfe,
Betwene your yong neighbour and his old ryche wyfe.

As

40

As this tale in this yong poore couple dooth ſhow,
And that the moſt good or leaſt yll ye know.
To take at ende, I was at begynnyng bent,
With thanks for this, and your more peyne to preuent,
Without any more matter now reuolued.
I take this matter here cléerely reſolued.
And that ye herein awarde me to forſake,
Beggerly beautie, and riueld riches take.
Thats iuſt, if the halfe ſhall iudge the whole (quoth I)
But yet here the whole, the whole wholly to try.
To it (quoth he) than I praie you by and by.
We will dyne fyrſt (quoth I) it is noone hy.
We maie as well (quoth he) dine whan this is doone.
The longer forenoone the ſhorter after noone.
All comth to one, and therby men haue geſt,
Alwaie the longer eaſt the ſhorter weſt.
We haue had (quoth I) before ye came, and fyn,
Weather, méete to ſette paddockes abroode in.
Rain, more than enough, and when all ſhrews haue dind,
Chaunge from foule weather to faire is oft enclind.
And all the ſhrews in this parte, ſauyng one wife
That muſt dine with vs, haue dinde peine of my life.
Now if good chaunge of ill weather be dependyng
Vpon hir diet, what were mine offendyng,
To kepe the woman any longer faſtyng.
If ye (quoth he) ſet all this far caſtyng,
For common wealth, as it apéereth a cléere caſe,
Reaſon would your will ſhuld, and ſhall take place.

¶Thus endeth the fyrſt part.

F   The

41

The seconde parte.

The. i. chapiter.

Diners can not be long, where deinties want,
  Where coine is not common, commons muſt be ſcant.
In poſte paſe we paſt from potage to chéeſe,
And yet this man cride, alas what time we léeſe.
He would not let vs pauſe after our repaſte,
But apart he pluckt me ſtreight, and in all haſte,
As I of this poore yonge man, and poore yong mayde,
Or more poore yong wyfe, the foreſaid woordes had ſaid,
So praieth he me now the proceſſe maie be tolde,
Betwéene thother yong man, and riche widow olde.
If ye lacke that (quoth I) awaie ye muſt wynde,
With your hole errand, and halfe thanſwere behynde.
Whiche thing to do, ſens haſt therto ſhewth you loth,
And to haſt your goyng, the daie awaie goth.
And that tyme loſte, again we can not wyn.
Without more loſſe of tyme, this tale I begyn.
   IN this late olde wydow, and than olde new wyfe,
Age and appetite fell at a ſtronge ſtryfe.
Her luſt was as yonge as hir lymis were olde.
The daie of hir weddyng, like one to be folde,
She ſet out hir ſelfe in fyne apparell.
She was made lyke a béere pot, or a barell.
A crooked hooked noſe, béetyll browde, blere eyde.
Many men wiſhte, for beautſiyng that bryde.
Hir waſte to be gyrde in, and for a boone grace,
Some well fauourd vyſor, on hir yll fauourd face.
But with viſorlyke viſage, ſuche as it was.
She ſmirkt, and ſhe ſmylde, but ſo liſped this las,
That folke might haue thought it doone onely alone,
Of wantonneſſe, had not hir téeth béene gone.

Vpright

Vpright as a candle ſtandth in a ſocket,
Stoode ſhe that daie, ſo ſimpre de cocket.
Of auncient fathers ſhe tooke no cure nor care,
She was to them, as koy as a crokers mare.
She tooke thenterteinment of the yong men
All in daliaunce, as nice as a nuns hen.
I ſuppoſe that daie hir eares might well glow,
For all the towne talkt of hir hy and low.
One ſaide, a well fauourd old woman ſhe is.
The diuell ſhe is ſaide an other. and to this,
In came the thyrde, with his. v. egges, and ſayde,
Fyfty yere ago I knew hir a trym mayde.
What euer ſhe were than (ſayd one) ſhe is nowe,
To become a bryde, as méete as a ſowe
To beare a ſaddle. She is in this mariage
As comely as is a cowe in a cage.
Gup with a galde backe gill, come vp to ſupper.
What mine olde mare woulde haue a new crouper.
And now mine olde hat muſt haue a new band.
Well (quoth one) glad is he that hath hir in hand.
A goodly maryage ſhe is, I here ſaie.
She is ſo (quoth one) were the woman awaie.
Well (quoth an other) fortune this moueth.
And in this caſe euery man as he loueth
Quoth the good man, whan that he kyſt his coowe.
That kyſſe (quoth one) doth well here, by god a voowe.
But how can ſhe geue a kyſſe ſowre or ſwéete ?
Her chin and hir noſe, within halfe an inche méete.
God is no botcher ſyr, ſaide an other.
He ſhapeth all partes, as eche part maie fytte other.
Well (quoth one) wiſely, let vs leaue this ſcannyng.
God ſpéede them. be as be maie is no bannyng.
That ſhalbe, ſhalbe. and with gods grace they ſhall
Doo well, and that they ſo may, wiſhe we all.

F ij

This

The second parte.

THIS wonder (as wonders laft) lafted nine daies.
Whiche doone, and all gefts of this feaft gon their waies,
Ordinary houfholde this man ftreight began.
Very fumptuoufly, whiche he might well doo than.
What he would haue, he might haue, his wife was fet
In fuche dotage of him, that fayre woordes did fet,
Gromelféede plentie, and pleafure to prefer,
She made muche of him, and he mockt muche of her.
I was (as I faide) muche there, and moft of all
The fyrft month in which time fuche kindneffe did fall,
Betwene thefe two counterfaite turtle burdes,
To fée his fwéete lookes, and here hir fwéete wurdes.
And to thinke wherfore they bothe put both in vre,
It wolde haue made a hors breake his halter fure.
All the fyrft fortnight their tickyng might haue tought,
Any yonge couple, their loue tickes to haue wrought.
Some laught, and faid, all thing is gay that is gréene.
Some therto faid, the gréene new brome fwéepth cléene.
But fens all thyng is the woors for the wearyng,
Decaie of cleane fwéepyng folke had in fearyng.
And in déede, er two monthes away were crept,
And hir biggeft baggs into his bofome fwept.
Where loue had apéered in him to hir alway
Hotte as a tofte, it grew cold as a kay.
He at meate caruyng hir, and none els before,
Now carued he to all but hir, and hir no more.
Where her woordes féemd hony, by his fmylyng chéere,
Now are they muftard, he frowneth them to héere.
And whan fhe fawe fwéete fauce began to waxe foure,
She waxt as fowre as he, and as well could lowre.
So turned they their typpets by way of exchaunge,
From laughyng to lowryng, and taunts did fo raunge,
That in plaine termes, plaine truth to you to vtter,
They two agréed like two cats in a gutter.

Mary

44

Mary fir (quoth he) by scratchyng and bytyng
Catts and dogs come together, by folkes recityng.
Together by the eares they come (quoth I) chéerely.
How be it thofe woords are not voyde here cléerely.
For in one ftate they twayne could not yet fettle.
But waueryng as the wynde, in docke out nettle.
Now in now out. now here now there, now fad.
Now mery, now hie, now lowe, now good, now bad.
In whiche vnftedy fturdy ftormes ftreinable.
To know how they bothe were irrefreynable,
Marke how they fell out, and how they fell in.
At ende of a fupper fhe did thus begin.

The. ii. chapiter.

HUfbande (quoth fhe) I would we were in our neft.
Whan the bealy is full, the bones wold be at reft.
So foone vpon fupper (faide he) no queftion,
Sléepe maketh yll and vnholfome digeftion,
By that diete a great difeafe once I gat.
And burnt childe fyre dredth. I will beware of that.
What a poft of phifyke (faide fhe) ye a poft.
And from poft to pyller wyfe, I haue béene toft
By that furfet. And I féele a little fyt,
Euen now, by former attemptyng of it.
Wherby, except I fhall féeme to leaue my wit,
Before it leaue me, I muft now leaue it.
I thanke God (quoth fhe) I neuer yet felt payne,
To go to bed timely, but rifyng againe
To foone in the mornyng, hath me difpleafed,
And I (quoth he) haue béene more difeafed,
By earely liyng downe, than by early rifyng.
But thus differ folke lo, in exercifyng.
That one may not, an other may.
Vfe maketh maiftry, and men many tymes fay,

F iij   That

That one loueth not, an other doth, which hath fped,
All meates to be eaten, and all maides to be wed.
Hafte ye to bed now, and ryfe ye as ye rate.
While I ryfe early, and come to bed late.
Long liyng warme in bed is holfome (quoth fhée)
While the leg warmeth, the boote harmeth (quoth hée)
Well (quoth fhe) he that dooth as moft men doo,
Shalbe leaft wondred on, and take any twoo,
That be man and wyfe in all this whole towne,
And mofte parte together, they ryfe and lie downe.
Whan byrds fhall rouft (quoth he) at. viii. ix. or ten,
Who fhall appoynt their houre, the cocke, or the hen.
The hen (quoth fhe) the cocke (quoth he) iuft (quoth fhe)
As Iermans lips. It fhall proue more iuft (quoth he)
Than proue I (quoth fhe) the more foole far away.
But there is no foole to the olde foole, folke fay.
Ye are wife inough (quoth he) if ye kéepe ye warme,
To be kept warme, and for none other harme,
Nor for muche more good, I tooke you to wedde.
I toke not you (quoth he) nyght and day to bedde.
Her carrain carkas (faide he) is fo colde,
Becaufe fhe is aged, and fomwhat to olde,
That fhe kylth me, I doo but rofte a ftone.
In warmyng hir. And fhall not I faue one,
As fhe wolde faue an other? yes by feint Iohne.
A fyr (quoth fhe) mary this geare is alone.
Who that woorft maie, fhall holde the candell, I fée,
I muft warme bed for him fhould warme it for mée.
This medicine thus miniftred is fharpe and colde.
But all thing that is fharpe is fhort. folke haue tolde.
This trade is now begun, but if it holde on,
Then farewell my good daies. they wyll be foone gon.
Gofpell in thy mouth (quoth he) this ftrife to breake.
How be it, all is not gofpell that thou doeft fpeake.

But

But what néede we lumpe out loue at ones laſhyng.
As we ſhould now ſhake handes. what ſoft for daſhyng.
The fayre laſteth all the yere. we be new knéet,
And ſo late met, that I feare we parte not yéet,
Quoth the baker to the pylorie. Which thyng,
From diſtemperate fondyng, temperance maie bryng.
And this reaſon to ayde, and make it more ſtrong,
Olde wiſe folke ſaie, loue me little, loue me long.
I ſay little (ſaid ſhe) but I thinke more.
Thought is frée. Ye leane (quoth he) to the wrong ſhore.
Braulyng booted not, he was not that night bent,
To plaie the bridgroome. Alone to bed ſhe went.
This was their beginnyng of iar. How be it,
For a begynnyng, this was a feat fit.
And but a fleabytyng to that did enſew.
The woorſt is behynd. we come not where it grew.
How ſay you (ſaid he to me) by my wyfe.
The diuell hath caſt a bone (ſaid I) to ſet ſtryfe
Betwéene you, but it were a foly for mée,
To put my hande betwéene the barke and the trée.
Or to put my finger to far in the fyre,
Betwéene you, and lay my credence in the myre.
To meddle little for me it is beſte.
For of little medlyng cometh great reſte.
Yes ye maie meddle (quoth he) to make hir wyfe,
Without takyng harme, in geuyng your aduiſe.
She knowth me not yet, but if ſhe waxe to wilde,
I ſhall make hir knowe, an olde knaue is no childe.
Sluggyng in bed with hir is woorſe than watchyng.
I promiſe you an olde ſacke axeth much patchyng.
Well (quoth I) to morowe I will to my beades,
To pray, that as ye both will, ſo ake your heades.
And in meane time my akyng head to eaſe,
I will couche a hogs hed. Quoth he whan ye pleaſe.

We

47

We parted, and this within a daie or twayne,
Was raakt vp in thafhes, and couerd agayne.

The. iii. chapiter.

THefe two daies paft, he faid to me, whan ye will,
Come chat at home, al is wel. Iack fhall haue gill.
Who had the wurs ende of the ftaffe (quoth I) now?
Shall the maifter weare a bréeche, or none? fay you.
I truft the fow will no more fo déepe wroote.
But if fhe doo (quoth he) you muft fet in foote.
And whom ye fée out of the waie, or fhoote wyde.
Ouer fhoote not your felfe any fyde to hyde.
But fhoote out fome woordes, if fhe be to whot.
She maie faie (quoth I) a fooles bolte foone fhot.
Ye will me to a thankeleffe office héere.
And a bufy officer I maie appéere.
And Iack out of office fhe maie bid me walke.
And thinke me as wife as Waltams calfe, to talke.
Or chat of hir charge, hauyng therin nought to doo,
How be it, if I fée néede, as my part comth too,
Gladly betwene you I will doo my beft.
I byd you to diner (quoth he) as no gefte,
And brynge your poore neighbors on your other fyde.
I did fo. And ftreight as tholde wife vs efpied,
She bad vs welcome and merily toward me,
Gréene rufhes for this ftraunger, ftrawe here (quoth fhe)
With this aparte fhe puld me by the fléeue.
Saiyng in few woords, my mynd to you to méeue,
So it is, that all our great fraie the laft night,
Is forgeuen and forgotten betwene vs quight.
And all fraies by this I truft haue taken end.
For I fully hope my hufband will amend.
Well amended (thought I) whan ye both relent,
Not to your owne, but eche to others mendment.

Now

48

Now if hope fayle (quoth fhe) and chaunce bryng about
Any fuche breache, wherby we fall again out.
I pray you tell him his pars vers now and than.
And winke on me alfo hardly, if ye can
Take me in any tryp. Quoth I, I am lothe,
To meddle commonly. For as this tale gothe,
Who medleth in all thyng, maie fhooe the goflyng,
Well (quoth fhe) your medlyng herein may bryng
The wynde calme betwéene vs, whan it els might rage.
I will with good will (quoth I) yll wynds to fwage,
Spend fom wind at néede, though I waft winde in vayne.
To table we fat, where fyne fare did remayne.
Mery we were as cup and can could holde,
Eche one with eche other homely and bolde.
And fhe for hir parte, made vs chéere heauen hye.
The fyrft parte of dyner mery as a pye.
But a fcalde head is foone broken. and fo they,
As ye fhall ftreight here, fell at a new frey.

The. iiii. chapiter.

HUfband (quoth fhe) ye ftudie, be mery now.
And euen as ye thynke now fo come to yow.
Nay not fo (quoth he) for my thought to tell right,
I thynke how ye lay gronyng wife, all laft night.
Hufband, a gronyng horfe, and a gronyng wyfe,
Neuer fayle their maifter (quoth fhe) for my lyfe.
No wyfe, a woman hath nyne lyues like a cat.
Well my lambe (quoth fhe) ye may picke out of that,
As foone goth the yonge lamfkyn to the market
As tholde yewes. God forbyd wyfe, ye fhall fyrft iet.
I will not iet yet (quoth fhe) put no doutyng.
It is a bad facke that will abide no cloutyng.
And as we oft fée, the lothe ftake ftandeth longe,
So is it an yll ftake I haue heard among.

G   That

49

That can not ſtande one yere in a hedge.
I drinke (quoth ſhe) Quoth he I will not pledge.
What nede all this, a man may loue his houſe well,
Though he ryde not on the rydge, I haue heard tell.
What, I wene (quoth ſhe) proferd ſeruyce ſtynkth.
But ſomwhat it is, I ſée, when the cat wynkth,
And bothe hir eyne out, but further ſtryfe to ſhonne,
Let the cat winke, and leat the mouſe ronne.
This paſt, and he chered vs all, but moſt chéere
On his part, to this fayre yong wyfe dyd appéere.
And as he to her caſt oft a louyng eye,
So caſt hir huſbande lyke eye, to his plate by.
Wherwith in a great muſyng he was brought.
Fréend (quoth the good man) a peny for your thought.
For my thought (quoth he) that is a goodly diſhe.
But of trough I thought, better to haue then wiſhe.
What, a goodly yong wyfe, as you haue (quoth he)
Nay (quoth he) goodly gylt goblets, as here bée.
Byr lady fréendis (quoth I) this maketh a ſhow,
To ſhewe you more vnnaturall than the crow,
The crow thinkth hir owne birdes faireſt in the wood.
But by your woordis (except I wrong vnderſtood)
Eche others byrdes or iewels, ye dooe weie
Aboue your owne. True (quoth the old wyfe) ye ſeie.
But my neighbours deſyre rightly to meaſure,
Comth of néede, and not of corrupte pleaſure.
And my huſbandis more of pleaſure, than of néede.
Olde fiſh and yong fleſh (quoth he) dooth men beſt féede.
And ſome ſay, chaunge of paſture makth fat calues.
As for that reaſon (quoth ſhe) ronth to halues.
As well for the coowe calfe as for the bull.
And though your paſture looke barreinly and dull,
Yet looke not on the meate, but looke on the man.
And who ſo looketh on you, ſhall ſhortly ſkan,

Ye

Ye maie wryte to your fréendis, that ye are in helth.
But all thyng maie be fuffred fauyng welth.
An olde faide fawe, itche and eafe, can no man pleafe.
Plentie is no deintie, ye fée not your owne eafe.
I fée, ye can not fée the wood for trées.
Your lips hang in your light, but this poore man fées
Both how blindly ye ftand in your owne light,
And that you rofe on your right fyde here right.
And might haue gone further, and haue faren wurs.
I wot well I might (quoth he) for the purs,
But ye be a baby of Belfabubs bowre.
Content ye (quoth fhe) take the fwéete with the fowre.
Fancy may boult bran, and make ye take it floure,
It will not be (quoth he) fhould I dye this houre.
While this fayre floure flourifheth thus in mine eye.
Yes, it might (quoth fhe) and here this reafon whye.

Snow is white *And lyeth in the dike*	*And euery man lets it lye.*
Pepper is blacke *And hath a good fmacke*	*And euery man doth it bye.*
Mylke (q' he) is white *And lieth not in the dike*	*But all men know it good meate.*
Inke is all blacke *And hath an ill fmacke*	*No man will it drinke nor eate.*

Thy ryme (quoth he) is muche elder then mine.
But myne beyng newer is truer then thine.
Thou likeneft now for a vayne aduauntage,
White fnow to fayre youth, blacke pepper to foule age.
Whiche are placed out of place here by rood.
Blacke inke is as yll meate, as blacke pepper is good.
And white milke as good meate, as white fnow is yll.
But a milke fnow white fmooth yong fkyn, who chaunge wil.
For a pepper ynke blacke rough olde wytherd face?
Though chaunge be no robbry for the chaunged cafe,

G ij   Yet

Yet ſhall that chaunge rob the chaunger of his wit.
For who this caſe ſercheth, ſhall ſoone ſée in it,
That as well agréeth thy compariſon in theſe,
As a lyke to compare in taſte, chalke and cheſe.
Or a like in colour to déeme ynke and chalke.
Walke drab walke. Nay (quoth ſhe) walke knaue walke
Saieth that terme. How be it ſir, I ſaie not ſo.
And beſt we laie a ſtrawe here, and euen there who.
Or els this geare will bréede a pad in the ſtrawe.
If ye hale this waie, I will an other waie drawe.
Here is God in thambrie (quoth I.) Quoth he, naie,
Here is the diuell in thorologe, ye maie ſaie.
Sens this (quoth I) rather bryngeth bale then boote,
Wrap it in the clothe, and tread it vnder foote.
Ye harpe on the ſtryng, that geueth no melody.
Your tounges run before your witis, by ſeint Antonie.
Marke ye, how ſhe hitteth me on the thombis (quoth hée)
And ye taunt me tyt ouer thumb (quoth ſhée)
Sens tyt for tat (quoth I) on euen hand is ſet,
Set the hares head againſt the gooſe ieblet.
She is (quoth he) bent to force you perfors
To know, that the grey mare is the better hors.
She chopth logyke, to put me to my clargy.
She hath one poynt of a good hauke, ſhe is hardie.
But wife, the fyrſt point of haukyng is holde faſt.
And holde ye faſt I red you, leſt ye be caſt,
In your owne tourne. Naie ſhe will tourne the leafe.
And rather (quoth I) take as ſalth in the ſheafe,
At your handes . and let fall hir holde, than be to bolde.
Naie, I will ſpyt in my handes, and take better holde.
He (quoth ſhe) that will be angry without cauſe,
Muſt be at one, without amendes . by ſage ſawes.
Tread a woorme on the tayle, and it muſt turne agayne.
He taketh pepper in the noſe, that I complaine

Vpon

52

Vpon his fautes, my felfe beyng fautleffe.
But that fhall not ftop my mouth, ye maie well geffe.
Well (quoth I) to muche of one thyng is not good,
Leaue of this. Be it (quoth he) fall we to our food.
But fuffrance is no quittance in this daiment.
No (quoth fhe) nor mifrecknyng is no paiment.
But euen recknyng maketh longe fréendis, my fréend.
For alwaie owne is owne, at the recknyngis éend.
This recknyng thus reckned, and dyner once doone,
We thrée from them twayne, departed very foone.

The. v. chapiter.

THis olde woman the next daie after this night,
Stale home to me, fecretly as fhe might.
To talke with me. In fecrete counfell (fhe faide)
Of thinges which in no wife might be bewraied.
We twayne are one to many (quoth I) for men fay,
Thrée maie a kepe counfayle, if two be away.
But all that ye fpeake, vnméete againe to tell,
I will fay nought but mum, and mum is counfell.
Well then (quoth fhe) herein auoydyng all feares,
Auoyd your children. fmall pitchers haue wide eares.
Whiche doone (fhe faide) I haue a hufband, ye know,
Whom I made of nought, as the thing felf dooth fhow.
And for thefe two caufes onely him I tooke.
Firft, that for my loue, he fhould louingly looke,
In all kynd of caufe, that loue ingender might,
To loue and cherifhe me by daie and by night.
Secondly, the fubftance, whiche I to him brought,
He rather fhould augment, than bring to nought,
But now my good, fhall both be fpent, ye fhall fée,
And it in fpendyng foole inftrument fhall bee
Of my deftruction, by fpendyng it on fuche
As fhall make him deftroy me; I feare this muche.

He maketh hauok. and setteth cocke on the hoope.
He is so laueis, the stocke beginneth to droope.
And as for gaine is deade, and layde in tumbe,
Whan he should get ought, eche synger is a thumbe,
Eche of his iointes against other iustles,
As handsomly as a beare picketh muscles.
Flattryng knaues & fleryng queanes beyng the marke.
Hang on his sléeue, many handis make light warke.
He hath his haukes in the mew. but make ye sure,
With emptie handes men maie no haukes allure.
There is a nest of chickens, whiche he dooth brood,
That will sure make his heare grow through his hood.
They can currifauell, and make faire wether,
Whyle they cut large thongis of other mens lether.
He maketh his marts with marchantis likely,
To bryng a shillyng to. ix. pens quickely.
If he holde on a while, as he begins,
We shall sée him proue a marchaunt of éele skins.
A marchaunt without either money or ware.
But all be bugs woords, that I speake to spare.
Better spare at brym than at bottem, say I.
Euer spare and euer bare (saith he) by and by.
Spend, and god shall send (saieth he) saith tholde ballet,
What sendth he (saie I) a staffe and a wallet.
Than vp gothe his staffe, to send me a loufe.
He is at thrée woordis vp in the house roufe.
And herein to grow (quoth she) to conclusion,
I praie your ayde, to auoid this confusion.
And for counsaile herein, I thought to haue gon,
To that cunnyng man, our curate sir Iohn.
But this kept me backe, I haue herd now and then,
The greattest clerkes be not the wysest men.
I thynk (quoth I) who euer that terme began,
Was neither great clerke, nor the greatest wise man.

In

In your rennyng from him to me, ye runne
Out of gods bleſſing into the warme ſunne.
Where the blynd leadth the blynd, both fall in the dike,
And blynde be we both, if we thinke vs his lyke.
Folke ſhow much foly, when things ſhould be ſped.
To ren to the foote, that maie go to the hed.
Sens he beſt can and moſt ought to dooe it,
I feare not, but he will, if ye wyll woo it.
There is one let (quoth ſhe) mo than I ſpake on.
My huſband and he be ſo great, that the ton
Can not piſſe, but the tother muſt let a fart.
Chooſe we him aparty, than farewell my part.
We ſhall ſo part ſtake, that I ſhall leſe the hole.
Folke ſay of olde, the ſhoe will holde with the ſole.
Shall I truſt him then? nay in truſt is treaſon.
But I truſt you, and come to you this ſeaſon
To here me, and tell me, what waie ye thinke beſt,
To hem in my huſbande, and ſet me in reſt.
If ye minde (quoth I) a conqueſt to make
Ouer your huſband, no man maie vndertake
To bryng you to eaſe, nor the matter amende.
Except ye bring him to weare a cocks comb at ende,
For take that your huſband were, as ye take him,
As I take him not, as your tale would make him.
Yet were contencion lyke to do nought in this,
But kepe him nought, and make him woors then he is,
But in this complaint, for counſele quicke and cléere,
A few prouerbes for principles, leat vs héere.
Who that maie not as they wolde, will as they maie.
And this to this, they that are bound muſt obaie:
Foly it is to ſpourne againſt a pricke,
To ſtryue againſt the ſtreme, to winche or kicke
Againſt the hard wall. By this ye maie ſée.
Beyng bound to obedience, as ye bee.

And

And alſo ouermacht, ſuffraunce is your daunce.
He maie ouermatche me (quoth ſhe) perchaunce
In ſtrength of bodie, but my tung is a lym,
To matche and to vexe euery vayne of him.
Toung breaketh bone, it ſelfe hauying none (quoth I)
If the winde ſtande in that dóore, it ſtandth awry.
The perill of pratyng out of tune by note,
Telth vs, that a good beſtyll is woorth a grote.
In beyng your owne foe, you ſpin a fayre thréede.
Aduyſe ye well, for here dooth all ly and bléede,
Flée thattemtyng of extremities all.
Folke ſaie, better ſyt ſtyll than ryſe and fall.
For little more or leſſe no debate make,
At euery dogs barke, ſéeme not to awake.
And where the ſmall with the great, can not agrée,
The weaker goeth to the potte, we all daie ſée.
So that alwaie the bygger eateth the beane.
Ye can nought wyn, by any wayward meane.
Where the hedge is loweſt, men maie ſooneſt ouer,
Be ſilent. Leat not your toung roon at rouer.
Sens by ſtryſe, ye maie loſe, and can not wyn,
Suffer. It is good ſlepyng in a whole ſkyn.
If he chide, kepe you byll vnder wyng muet.
Chatting to chiding is not woorth a chuet.
We ſée many tymes, might ouercomth right.
Were not you as good than to ſay, the crow is whight.
And ſo rather let faire woordes make fooles fayne,
Than be plaine without pletes, & plant your owne payne.
For were ye as plaine as dunſtable by waie.
Yet ſhould ye that waie rather breake a loue daie,
Than make one thus though ye perfytely knew,
All that ye coniecture to be proued trew,
Yet better diſſemble it, and ſhake it of,
Than to broide him with it in earneſt or ſcof.

If

If he plaie falſehed in felowſhip, plaie yée,
Sée me, and ſée me not. to woorſt part to flée.
Why thinke ye me ſo whyte lyuerd (quoth ſhée)
That I will be toung tyed? Naie I warrant yée.
They that will be afraid of euery farte,
Muſt go far to piſſe. Well (quoth I) your parte
Is to ſuffre (I ſaie) For ye ſhall préeue.
Tauntis appeaſe not thingis, they rather agréeue,
But for yll company, or expenſe extréeme,
I here no man doubte, ſo far as ye déeme.
And there is no fyre without ſome ſmoke, we ſée.
Well well, make no fyre, reyſe no ſmoke (ſayd ſhée)
What cloke for the rayne ſo euer ye bryng mée,
My ſelfe can tell beſt, where my ſhooe doth wryng mée.
But as ye ſaie, where fyre is, ſmoke will appéere.
And ſo hath it doone, For I did lately héere,
How flek and his make, vſe their ſecrete hauntyng,
By one byrd, that in mine eare was late chauntyng.
One ſwalowe maketh not ſommer (ſaid I) men ſaie.
I haue (quoth ſhe) mo blockis in his waie to laie.
For further encreaſe of ſuſpicion of yls,
Beſyde his iettyng into the towne, to his gyls,
With calets he conſumeth him ſelfe and my goodes,
Sometyme in the féelds, ſometyme in the woodes.
Some here and ſée him, whom he hereth nor ſéeth not.
But féelds haue eies, and woodes haue eares, ye wot.
And alſo on my maydes he is euer tootyng.
Can ye iudge a man (quoth I) by his lookyng?
What, a cat maie looke on a king, ye know.
My cats léeryng looke (quoth ſhe) at fyrſt ſhow.
Shewth me, that my cat gothe a catterwawyng.
And ſpecially by his maner of drawyng,
To Madge my faire maide. for may he come ny her.
He muſt nedes baſſe hir, as he comth by her.

H   He

He loueth well fhéeps flefh, that wets his bred in the wul,
If he leaue it not, we haue a crow to pul.
He loueth hir better at the fole of the foote,
Than euer he loued me at the hert roote.
It is a foule byrd, that fyleth his owne nest.
I wold haue him liue as gods lawe hath expreft.
And leaue lewde tickyng. he that will none ill doo.
Muft do nothyng, that belongeth therto.
To ticke and laughe with me, he hath laufull leeue.
To that I faide nought but laught in my fleeue.
But whan fhe féemed to be fixed in mynde,
Rather to féeke for that fhe was lothe to fynde,
Than leaue that féekyng, by whiche fhe might fynd eafe,
I fainde this fancy to féele how it would pleafe
Will ye do well (quoth I) take peyne to watche him.
And if ye chaunce in aduoutrie to catche him,
Then haue ye him on the hyp, or on the hyrdell.
Then haue ye his head faft vnder your gyrdell.
Where your wurds now do but rub him on the gall.
That déede without woords fhall driue him to the wall.
And further than the wall he can not go.
But muft fubmit him felfe, and if it hap fo,
That at ende of your watche, he gyltles apéere,
Then all grudge, growne by ielowfie, taketh end cléere.
Of all folkes I maie woorft watche him (faid fhe)
For of all folks him felfe moft watcheth me.
I fhall as foone trie him or take him this waie,
As dryue a top ouer a tyeld houfe, no naie.
I maie kepe corners or holowe trées with thowle,
This feuen yeres, daie and night to watche a bowle.
Before I fhall catche him with vndoubted euill.
He muft haue a long fpoone, fhall eate with the diuell.
And the deuill is no falfer then is hée.
I haue heard tell, it had néede to bée.

A

A wyly moufe that fhould bréede in the cats eare.
Shall I get within him than? nay ware that geare.
It is harde haltyng before a créeple ye wot.
A falfer water drinker there liueth not.
Whan he hunteth a doe, that he can not avow,
All dogs barke not at him, I warrant yow.
Namely not I, I faie, though as I fayde.
He fomtyme, though feldome, by fome be bewrayde.
Clofe huntyng (quoth I) the good hunter alowth.
But be your hufband neuer fo ftyll of mouth,
If ye can hunt, and will ftand at receite.
Your maide examinde, maketh him open ftreite.
That were (quoth fhe) as of my truth to make préefe,
To axe my felow whether I be a théefe.
They cleaue together like burs. that way I fhall
Pike out no more, than out of the ftone wall.
Than lyke ye not to watche him for wife nor mayde.
No (quoth fhe) Nor I (quoth I) what euer I fayde.
And I miflyke not onely your watche in vayne.
But alfo if ye tooke him. what could ye gayne?
From fufpicion to knowlage of yll. forfoothe
Coulde make ye dooe, but as the flounder doothe,
Leape out of the friyng pan into the fyre.
And chaunge from yll peyn to wurs is worth fmall hyre.
Let tyme trie. Tyme tryeth trouth in euery doubt.
And déeme the beft, till time hath tryde the trouth out.
And reafon faieth, make not two forowes of one,
But ye make ten forowes where reafon maketh none.
For where reafon (as I faide) wylth you to winke,
(Although all were proued as yll as ye thinke)
Contrary to reafon ye ftampe and ye ftare.
Ye fret and ye fume as mad as a marche hare.
Without proofe to his reproofe prefent or paft.
But by fuche reporte, as mofte proue lies at laft.

H ij

And

And here gothe the hare awaie, for ye iudge all,
And iudge the woorſt in all, er proofe in ought fall.
But blinde men ſhould iudge no colours: by olde ſauſe,
And folk oft tymes ar moſt blind in their owne cauſe,
The blynde eate many flies. Howbeit the fancy,
Of your blindneſſe comth not of ignorancy.
Ye coulde tell an other herein the beſt waie.
But it is as folke dooe, and not as folke ſaie.
For they ſaie, ſaiyng and dooyng are two thingis,
To defende daunger that double dealyng brynges.
As ye can ſéeme wiſe in woords, be wiſe in déede.
That is (quoth ſhe) ſooner ſaid then doone, I dréede.
But me thinkth your counſell weith in the whole,
To make me put my fynger in a hole.
And ſo by ſuffrance to be ſo lyther,
In my houſe to lay fyre and tow together.
But if they fyre me, ſome of them ſhall wyn
More towe on their diſtaues, than they can well ſpyn.
And the beſt of them ſhall haue both their handis full.
Bolſter or pillow for me, be whoſe wull.
I will not beare the diuels ſacke, by ſaint Audry.
For concelyng ſuſpicion of their baudry.
I feare fals meaſures, or els I were a chylde.
For they that thinke none yll, are ſooneſt begylde.
And thus though muche water goeth by the myll,
That the miller knowth not of, yet I will
Caſt what may ſcape, and as though I did fynde it.
With the clacke of my myll, to fyne meale grynde it.
And ſure ere I take any reſt in effect,
I muſt baniſhe my maydes ſuche as I ſuſpect.
Better it be doone than wiſhe it had bene doone.
As good vndoone (quoth I) as doo it to ſoone.
Well (quoth ſhe) till ſoone, fare ye well, and this
Kéepe ye as ſecrete, as ye thinke méete is.

                                                            Out

Out at doores went fhe herewith. and hereupon
In at doores came he foorthwith as fhe was gon.
And without any temprate proteftacion,
Thus he began, in waie of exclamacion.

The. vi. chapiter.

OH what choyce may compare, to the diuels lyfe,
Lyke his, that haue chofen a diuel to his wife?
Namely fuch an olde witche, fuche a mackabroyne,
As euermore like a hog hangeth the groyne,
On hir hufbande, except he be hir flaue,
And folow all fancies, that fhe would haue.
Tys fayde, there is no good accorde,
Where euery man would be a Lorde.
Wherfore my wyfe will be no lorde, but lady,
To make me, that fhould be her Lorde, a baby.
Before I was wedded, and fens, I made recknyng,
To make my wyfe boow at euery becknyng.
Bachelers boft, how they will teach their wyues good,
But many a man fpeaketh of Robyn hood,
That neuer fhot in his bowe. Whan all is fought,
Bachelers wiues, and maides children be well tought.
And this with this, I alfo begin to gather,
Euery man can rule a fhrewe, faue he that hath her.
At my wil I wend fhe fhould haue wrought, like wax.
But I fynde and féele, fhe hath found fuche knax
In her bouget, and fuche toies in her hed.
That to daunce after her pipe, I am ny led.
It is faide of olde, an olde dog byteth fore.
But by God, tholde bitche biteth forer and more.
And not with téeth (fhe hath none) but with hir toung.
If all tales be true (quoth I) though fhe be ftong,
And therby ftyng you, fhe is not muche to blame,
For what euer you faie. thus goeth the fame.

H iij

Whan

Whan folke firſt ſaw your ſubſtance layd in your lap,
Without your peyn, with your wife brought by good hap,
Oft in remembrance of haps happie deuiſe,
They would ſaie, better to be happie then wiſe.
Not minding therby than, to depraue your wit,
For they had good hope, to ſée good proofe of it.
But ſens their good opinion therin ſo cooles,
That they ſaie as ofte, God ſendeth fortune to fooles.
In that as fortune without your wit gaue it,
So can your wit not kéepe it whan ye haue it.
Saieth one, this geare was gotten on a holy daie.
Saieth an other, who maie holde that will awaie.
This game from begynnyng, ſhewth what ende is ment.
Soone gotten, ſoone ſpent, yll gotten yll ſpent.
Yé are calde not onely to great a ſpender,
To franke a geuer, and as frée a lender.
But alſo ye ſpende geue and lende, among ſuche,
Whoſe lightneſſe miniſheth your honeſtée as muche
As your money, and much they diſalow,
That ye bryke all from hir, that brought all to yow.
And ſpende it out at doores, in ſpyte of hir,
Becauſe ye wolde kyll hir to be quite of hir.
For all kindneſſe, of hir parte, that maie ryſe,
Ye ſhewe all thunkindneſſe ye can deuiſe.
And where reaſon and cuſtome (they ſay) afoords,
Alwaie to let the looſers haue their woords,
Ye make hir a cookqueane, and conſume hir good.
And ſhe muſt ſyt like a beane in a moonkis hood.
Bearyng no more rule, than a gooſe turd in tems,
But at hir owne maides becks, winges, or hems,
She muſt obey thoſe lambs, or els a lambs ſkyn,
Ye will prouyde for hir, to lap her in.
This biteth the mare by the thumbe, as they ſey.
For were ye, touching condicion (ſay they)

The

The caſtell of honeſtée in all things els.
Yet ſhould this one thing, as their hole tale tels,
Defoyle and deface that caſtell to a cotage.
One crop of a tourd marrth a pot of potage,
And ſome to this, crie, let him pas, for we thinke,
The more we ſtur a tourde, the wurs it will ſtynke,
With many condicions good, one that is yll,
Defaceth the flowre of all, and dooth all ſpyll.
Nowe (quoth I) if you thinke they truely clatter,
Let your amendment amende the matter.
Halfe warnd halfe armde. this warnyng for this I ſhow,
He that hath an yll name, is halfe hangd, ye know.

The. vii. chapiter.

VVell ſaide (ſaide he) mary ſir here is a tale,
For honeſtie, méete to ſet the diuell on ſale.
But now am I forſt, a bead roule to vnfolde,
To tell ſomwhat more to the tale I erſt tolde.
Grow this. as moſt part doth, I durſt holde my lyfe,
Of the ieloufy of dame Iulok my wyfe,
Than ſhall ye wonder, whan truth doth defyne,
How ſhe can, and doth here, both byte and whyne.
Franſy, hereſy, and ieloufy are thrée,
That men ſay hardly or neuer cured bée.
And although ieloufy néede not or boote not,
What helpeth that counſayle, if reaſon roote not.
And in mad ieloufy ſhe is ſo farre gon,
She thinkth I run ouer all, that I looke on.
Take good héede of that (quoth I) for at a woorde,
The prouerbe ſaith, he that ſtriketh with the ſwoorde,
Shalbe ſtrikyn with the ſcaberde. Tuſhe (quoth he)
The diule with my ſcaberde will not ſtrike me.
But my dame takyng ſuſpicion for full préefe,
Reporteth it for a trouth, to the moſte miſchéefe.

In

In woordis golde and hole, as men by wyt could wifhe.
She will lie as faft as a dogge will licke a difhe.
She is of trouth as fals, as God is trew.
And if fhe chaunce to fée me at a vew
Kyffe any of my maydes alone, but in fporte,
That taketh fhe in erneft. after Bedlem forte.
The cow is wood. Her tong ronth on patens.
If it be morne, we haue a payre of matens.
If it be euen, euenfong, not Laten nor Gréeke,
But Englifhe, and like thut as in eafter weeke.
She beginneth, firft with a cry a leyfone.
To whiche fhe ringth a peale, a larom. fuche one,
As folke ring bées with bafons. the world runth on whéeles.
But except hir maide fhewe a fayre paire of héeles,
She haleth her by the boy rope, tyll hir braines ake.
And bring I home a good difhe. good chéere to make,
What is this (faith fhe) Good meate (faie I) for yow.
God haue mercy hors, a pyg of mine owne fow.
Thus whan I fée, by kindneffe eafe renewth not,
And than, that the eie féeth not, the hert rewth not,
And that he muft néedes go, whom the diuel dooth driue,
Her force forcing me, for mine eafe to contriue,
To let her faft and freate alone for me,
I go where mery chat, and good chéere may be.
Muche fpend I abrode, whiche at home fhould be fpent,
If fhe would leaue controllyng, and be content.
There lepte a whityng (quoth fhe) and lept in ftreite.
Take a heare from his bearde, and marke this conceite.
He makth you beleue, by lies laide on by lode,
My braulyng at home, makith him banket abrode.
Where his bankets abrode, make me braule at home.
For as in a froft, a mud wall made of lome
Cracketh and crummeth in péeces a funder,
So melteth his money, to the worlds wonder.

So

64

Thus maie ye fée, to tourne the cat in the pan,
Or fet the cart before the hors, well he can.
He is but little at home, the trewth is fo.
And foorth with him, he will not let me go.
And if I come to be mery where he is,
Than is he mad. as ye fhall here by this.
Where he with goffyps at a banket late was,
At whiche as vfe is, he paide all. but let pas.
I came to be mery. wherwith merily,
Proface. Haue among you blynd harpers (fayde I)
The mo the merier, we all daie here and fée.
Ye, but the fewer the better fare (faid hée)
Then here were, er I came (quoth I) to many,
Here is but little meate lefte, if there be any.
And it is yll commyng, I haue heard fay,
To thend of a fhot, and beginnyng of a fray.
Put vp thy purs (quoth he) thou fhalt none paie.
And fray here fhould be none, were thou gone thy way.
Here is, fens thou camft, to many féete a bed.
Welcom when thou goeft. thus is thine errand fped.
I come (quoth I) to be one here, if I fhall,
It is mery in halle, when berds wag all.
What, byd me welcome pyg. I pray the kys me.
Nay farewell fow (quoth he) our lord blys me
From baffyng of beaftes of Beare binder lane.
I haue (quoth I) for fyne fuger, faire rats bane.
Many yeres fens, my mother faide to me,
Her elders would faie, it is better to be
An olde mans derlyng, than a yong mans werlyng.
And god knowth. I knew none of this fnerlyng
In my olde husfbandis daies. for as tenderly,
He loued me, as ye loue me fklenderly.
We drew both in one line. Quoth he wold to our lorde
Ve had in that drawyng, hangd both in one corde.

I   For

For I neuer méete the at flefhe nor at fifhe,
But I haue fure a deade mans head in my difhe.
Whofe beft and my woorft daie, that wifht might bée,
Was when thou didft bury him and mary mée.
If you (quoth I) long for chaunge in thofe cafes,
Wold to god he and you, had chaunged places.
But beft I chaunge place, for here I may be fparde.
And for my kynde commyng, this is my rewarde.
Claw a churle by thars, and he fhyteth in my hand.
Knak me that nut. much good doyt you all this band.
Muft fhe not (quoth he) be welcome to vs all,
Among vs all, lettyng fuche a farewell fall?
Suche carpenters, fuch chips. (quoth fhe) folke tell,
Suche lips, fuche lettice. fuch welcome, fuch farewell.
Thine owne woordis (quoth he) thine owne welcome mard.
Well (faide fhe) whan fo euer we twayne haue iard,
My woordis be pried at narowly, I efpie.
Ye can fée a mote in an other mans iye,
But ye can not fée a balke in your owne.
Ye marke my woordis, but not that they be growne,
By your reuellous rydyng on euery royle.
Well ny euery day a new mare or a moyle.
As muche vnhoneft, as vnprofytable.
Whiche fhall bryng vs fhortly to be vnable,
To geue a dog a lofe, as I haue oft faide.
Howe be it your pleafure maie no tyme be denayde.
But ftill you muft haue, bothe the fynest meate,
Apparail, and all thing that money maie geate,
Lyke one of fond fancy fo fyne and fo neate,
That would haue better bread than is made of wheate.
The beft is beft cheape (quoth he) men faie cléere.
Well (quoth fhe) a man may by gold to déere.
Ye nother care, nor welny caft what ye paie,
To by the dereft for the beft alwaie.

Than

Than for your diet who vſeth féedyng ſuch,
Eate more than enough, and drink much more to much.
But temprance teacheth this, where he kepeth ſcoole,
He that knoweth whan he hath enough, is no foole.
Féed by meaſure, and defie the phiſicion.
And in the contrary marke this condicion,
A ſwyne ouer fatte is cauſe of his owne bane.
Who ſéeth nought herein, his wit is in the wane.
But pompous prouiſion, comth not all, alway
Of glottony, but of pryde ſometyme, ſome ſay.
But this prouerbe precheth to men haute or hye,
Hewe not to hye, left the chips fall in thine iye.
Meaſure is a mery meane, as this doth ſhow,
Not to hye for the pye, nor to lowe for the crow.
The difference betwene ſtaryng and ſtarke blynde.
The wiſe man at all tymes to folow can fynde.
And ywis an auditour of a meane wit,
Maie ſoone accompt, though hereafter come not yit,
Yet is he ſure be the daie neuer ſo long,
Euermore at laſte they ryng to euenſong.
And where ye ſpend much though ye ſpent but lickell,
Yet littell and littell the cat eateth the flickell.
Little loſſe by length maie growe importable.
A mouſe in tyme, maie byte a two, a cable.
Thus to ende of all thingis, be we léefe or lothe,
Yet lo, the pot ſo long to the water gothe.
Tyll at the laſte it comthe home broken.
Fewe woordis to the wiſe ſuffice to be ſpoken.
If ye were wiſe, here were enough (quoth ſhée)
Here is enough, and to muche, dame (quoth he)
For though this appéere a proper pulpet péece,
Yet whan the fox preacheth, then beware your géeſe.
A good tale yll tolde, in the tellyng is marde.
So are (quoth ſhe) good tales well tolde, and yll harde.

I ij

Thy

Thy tales (quoth he) ſhew long heare, and ſhort wit, wife.
But long be thy legs, and ſhort be thy lyfe.
Pray for your ſelfe, I am not ſicke (quoth ſhe)
Well lets ſée, what thy laſt tale comth to (quoth he)
Thou ſaieſt I ſpend all, to this, thy woordis wander.
But as deepe drinketh the gooſe, as the gander.
Thou canſt cough in the aumbry, if néede bée,
Whan I ſhall cough without bread or broth for thée.
Wherby while thou ſendſt me abrode to ſpende.
Thou goſſepſt at home, to méete me at landis ende.
Ah, than I begyle you (quoth ſhe) this ye meane.
But ſyr, my pot is whole, and my water cleane.
Well, thou woldſt haue me (quoth he) pinch lyke a ſnudge,
Euery daie to be thy driuell and drudge.
Not ſo (quoth ſhe) but I would haüe ye ſtur
Honeſtly, to kepe the wolfe from the dur.
I wold driue the wulfe out at doore fyrſt (quoth he)
And that can I not doo, tyll I dryue out thée.
A man were better be drownde in Venice gulfe
Than haue ſuche a bearded beare, or ſuche a wulfe.
But had I not béene witcht, my weddyng to flée,
The termes that longe to weddyng had warnde mée.
Firſt wooyng for woing, banna for bannyng.
The banes for my bane, and than this thus ſcannyng,
Mariyng marryng. And what maryed I than?
A woman. As who ſaith, wo to the man.
Thus wed I with wo, wed I Gyll, wed I Iane.
I pray god the deuel go with the, downe the lane.
I graunt (quoth ſhe) this dooth ſound (as ye agréed)
On your ſyde in woordis, but on my ſyde in déede.
Thou grantſt this graunt (quoth he) without any grace,
Vngracioüſly, to thy ſyde, to tourne this caſe.
Leaue this (quoth ſhe) and learne liberalitée,
To ſtynt ſtryfe, growne by your prodigalitée.

                                                        Oft

Oft faid the wife man, whom I erft did bery,
Better are meales many, than one to mery.
Well (quoth he) that is anfwered with this wife.
Better is one monthes chéere, than a churles hole lyfe.
I thinke it learnyng of a wyfer lectour,
To learne to make my felfe myne owne exectour,
Than fpare for an other that might wed thée,
As the foole, thy fyrft hufband fpared for mée.
And as for yll places, thou fekeft me in mo,
And in woorfe to, than I into any go.
Wherby this prouerbe fhewth the in by the wéeke.
No man will an other in the ouen féeke,
Except that him felfe haue béene there before.
God geue grace thou haft béene good, I faie no more.
And wolde haue the fay leffe. except thou couldft proue
Suche proceffe as thou fclanderoufly doeft moue.
For fclaunder perchaunce (quoth fhe) I not denie.
It maie be a fclaunder, but it is no lie.
It is a lye (quoth he) and thou a lyer.
Will ye (quoth fhe) dryue me to touche ye nyer?
I rub the gald hors backe till he winche, and yit
He would make it féeme, that I touche him no whit
But I wot what I wot, though I few woordis make.
Many kiffe the childe for the nurfes fake.
Ye haue many god children to looke vpon,
And ye bleffe them all, but ye baffe but one.
This halfe fhewth, what the hole meaneth, that I méeue,
Ye fet circumquaques to make me beleue
Or thinke, that the moone is made of a gréene chéefe.
And whan ye haue made me a loute in all théefe,
It femeth ye wolde make me go to bed at noone.
Naie (quoth he) the daie of doome fhall be doone,
Er thou go to bed at noone or night for mée.
Thou art, to be plaine, and not to flatter thée,

As holſome a morſell for my comely cors.
As a ſhoulder of mutton for a ſicke hors.
The diuell with his dam, hath more reſt in hell,
Than I haue here with the. but well wiſ well.
Well well (quoth ſhe) many wels, many buckets.
Ye (quoth he) and many woords, many buffets.
Had you ſome huſband, and ſnapte at him thus,
Iwys he would geue you a recumbentibus.
A dog will barke er he bite, and ſo thow,
After thy barkyng wilt bite me, I trow now.
But it is harde to make an olde dog ſtoupe, lo.
Sir (quoth ſhe) a man maie handle his dog ſo,
That he maie make him byte him, though he would not,
Huſbandes are in heauen (quoth he) whoſe wiues ſcold not.
Thou makeſt me claw where it itcheth not. I would
Thy toung were coold to make thy tales more cold,
That aſpine leafe, ſuche ſpitefull clappyng haue bred.
That my cap is better at eaſe then my hed.
God ſende that hed (ſaid ſhe) a better nurs.
For whan the head aketh, all the bodie is the wurs.
God graunt (quoth I) the head and bodie both twoo.
To nourſe eche other, better then they doo.
Or euer haue doone for the moſte tymes paſte.
I brought to nurs both (quoth ſhe) had it not béene waſte.
Margery good coowe (quoth he) gaue a good méele,
But than ſhe caſt it downe again with hir héele.
Howe can hir purs for profite be delitefull?
Whoſe perſon and properties be thus ſpitefull.
A péece of a kyd is woorth two of a cat.
Who the diuell will chaunge a rabet for a rat?
If I might chaunge, I wolde rather chooſe to begge,
Or ſit with a roſted appull, or an egge,
Where mine appetite ſerueth me to bée,
Then euery daie to fare lyke a duke with thée.

Lyke

Lyke a duke, lyke a duck (quoth fhe) thou fhalt fare,
Except thou wilt fpare, more than thou doft yet fpare.
Thou fareft to well (quoth he) but thou art fo wood,
Thou knowft not who doth the harme, who doth the good.
Yes yes (quoth fhe) for all thofe wyfe woordis vttred,
I know on which fyde my bread is buttred.
But there will no butter cleaue on my breade.
And on my bread any butter to be fpreade.
Euery promife that thou therin doft vtter,
Is as fure as it were fealed with butter.
Or a moufe tied with a thréede. Euery good thyng,
Thou letteft euen flyp, lyke a waghalter flypftryng.
But take vp in time, or els I proteft,
All be not a bedde, that fhall haue yll reft.
Now go to thy derlyngis, and declare thy gréefe.
Where all thy pleafure is, hop hoore, pipe théefe.

The. viii. chapiter.

VVith this thence hopt fhe, whewith o lord he cryde,
What wretch but I, this wretchednes could byde.
Howe be it in all this wo, I haue no wrong
For it onely is all on my felfe along.
Where I fhould haue brydled her fyrft with rough bit,
To haue made hir chew on the brydell one fit.
For likorous lucre of a little wynnyng,
I gaue hir the brydell at begynnyng.
And now fhe taketh the brydell in the téeth,
And runth away with it, wherby eche man féeth,
It is (as olde men right well vnderftande)
Ill puttyng a nakt fwoord in a mad mans hande.
She takth fuch hert of grace, that though I maime hir.
Or kyll hir, yet fhall I neuer reclaime hir,
She hath (they fay) bene ftyffe necked euermore.
And it is yll healyng of an olde fore.

This

This prouerbe prophecied many yeres agone.
It will not out of the flefhe that is bred in the bone.
What chaunce haue I, to haue a wife of fuche fort,
That will no faute amend in earneft nor fport?
A fmall thinge amis lately I did efpy,
Whiche to make hir mende, by a ieft mirily,
I faidé but this, taunt tiuet wife, your nofe drops.
So it maie fall, I will eate no broweffe fops
This daie. But two daies after this came in vre,
I had forow to my fops ynough be fure.
Well (quoth I) it is yll ieftyng on the foothe.
Sooth bourd is no bourd, in ought that mirth doothe.
Suche ieftes could not iuggle hir, were ought amis.
Nor turne melancoly to myrth. for it is
No plaiyng with a ftrawe before an olde cat,
Euery tryflyng toie age can not laugh at.
Ye maie walke this waie, but fure ye fhall fynde,
The further ye go, the further behynde.
Ye fhould confyder the woman is olde.
And what for a whot woorde. Sone whot, fone colde.
Beare with them, that beare with you, and fhe is fcand,
Not onely the faireft floure in your garland,
But alfo fhe is all the faire flowers therof,
Will ye requyte hir then with a tauntyng fcof?
Or with any other kynd of vnkyndneffe?
Take héede is a faire thing. Beware this blindneffe.
Why will ye (quoth he) I fhall folow hir will?
To make me Iohn drawlache, or fuch a fnekebill.
To bryng hir folace, that bryngeth me forow,
Byr lady, than we fhall catche byrds to morow.
A good wife makth a good hufbande, (they faie)
That (quoth I) ye maie tourne an other waie.
To make a good hufband, make a good wyfe.
I can no more herin, but god ftint all ftrife.

Amen

72

Amen (quoth he) and god haue mercy brother,
I will now mend this houfe, and payre an other.
And that he ment of likelyhood by his owne.
For fo apairde he that, er thrée yeres were growne.
That little and little he decaied fo long,
Tyll he at length came to buckle and bare thong.
To difcharge charge, that neceffarily grew,
There was no more water than the fhip drew.
Suche driftes draue he, from yll to wars and wars,
Tyll he was as bare as a byrdes ars.
Money, and money woorth, did fo miffe him,
That he had not now one peny to bliffe him.
Whiche foreféene in this woman wifely waiyng,
That méete was to ftaie fomwhat for hir ftaiyng,
To kepe yet one meffe for Alifon in ftore,
She kept one bag, that he had not féene before.
A poore cooke that maie not licke his owne fyngers.
But about hir at home now ftill he lingers,
Not checker a boord, all was not cléere in the cofte,
He lookt lyke one that had befhyt the rofte.
But whether any fecrete tales were fprinklyng,
Or that he by geffe had got an inklyng
Of hir hoord. or that he thought to amend.
And tourne his yll begynnyng to a good ende.
In fhewyng him felfe a new man, as was féet,
That appéered fhortly after, but not yéet,

The. ix. chapiter.

ONe daie in their arbour, whiche ftoode fo to mine,
That I might and did clofely myne eare incline,
And likewyfe caft mine eye to here and fée,
What they faide and did, where they could not fée mée,
He vnto hir a goodly tale began,
More like a wooer, than a wedded man.

K

As

As ferre as matter therof therein ſerued,
But the fyrſt part from woordis of wooyng ſwerued,
And ſtood vpon repentaunce, with ſubmiſſion,
Of his former crooked vnkynde condicion.
Praiyng hir, to forgeue and forget all frée,
And he forgaue hir, as he forgeuen wolde bée.
Louyng hir now, as he full déepely ſwore,
As whotly as euer he loued hir before.
Well well (quoth ſhe) what euer ye now ſaie,
It is to late to call again yeſterdaie.
Wife (quoth he) ſuche maie my diligence féeme,
That thoffence of yeſterdaie I maie redéeme.
God taketh me as I am, and not as I was.
Take you me ſo to, and let all thinges paſt pas.
I praie the good wife, thinke I ſpeake and think plaine.
What, he runth far, that neuer turnth againe.
Ye be yong enough to mende, I agrée it,
But I am (quoth ſhe) to old to ſée it.
And amende ye or not, I am to olde a yere.
What is lyfe? where liuyng is extinct cléere.
Namely at olde yeres of leaſte helpe and moſt néede.
But no tale coulde tune you, in tyme to take héede.
If I tune my ſelfe now (quoth he) it is fayre.
And hope of true tune, ſhall tune me from diſpayre.
Beleue well, and haue well, men ſay. ye, (ſaid ſhée)
Doo well, and haue well, men ſay alſo, we ſée.
But what man can beleue, that man can do well,
Who of no man will counſell take or here tell.
Whiche to you, whan any man any way tryde,
Than were ye deafe, ye could not here on that ſyde.
Who euer with you any tyme therin weares,
He muſt both tell you a tale, and fynde you eares.
You had on your harueſt eares, thicke of hearyng.
But this is a queſtion of olde enqueryng,

Who

74

Who is so deafe, or so blynde, as is hée,
That wilfully will nother here nor sée?
Whan I saw your maner, my herte for wo molte.
Than wolde ye mend, as the fletcher mends his bolte.
Or as sowre ale mendth in summer, I know,
And knew, which waie the winde blewe, and will blow.
Though not to my profite, a prophete was I.
I prophecied this, to true a prophecie.
Whan I was right yll beleued, and worse hard.
By flingyng from your folkes at home, which all mard.
Whan I said in semblaunce eyther cold or warme,
A man far from his good, is nye his harme.
Or wilde ye to looke, that ye lost no more,
On suche as shewe, that hungry flies byte sore.
Than wold ye looke ouer me, with stomake swolne,
Like as the diuel lookt ouer Lincolne.
The diuell is dead wife (quoth he) for ye sée,
I looke lyke a lambe in all your woordis to mée.
Looke as ye list now (quoth she) thus lookt ye than.
And for those lookes I shew this, to shew eche man,
Suche proofe of this prouerbe, as none is gretter.
Which saith, that some man maie steale a hors better,
Than some other may stande and looke vpone.
Leude huswiues might haue woordis, but I not one
That might be aloude. But now if ye looke,
In mistakyng me, ye may sée, ye tooke
The wrong way to wood, and the wrong sow by theare.
And therby in the wrong boxe to thryue ye weare,
I haue heard some, to some tell this tale not féelde.
Whan thrift is in the towne, ye be in the féelde.
But contrary, you made that sence to sowne,
Whan thrift was in the féelde, ye were in the towne.
Féelde ware might sinke or swym, while ye had eny.
Towne ware was your ware, to tourne the peny.

K ij

But

75

But towne or féelde, where moſt thrift did apéere,
What ye wan in the hundred ye loſt in the ſhéere.
In all your good huſbandry, thus ryd the rocke,
Ye ſtumbled at a ſtrawe, and lept euer a blocke.
So many kyndes of increaſe you had in choice,
And nought increaſe nor kepe, how can I reioyce?
Good ridyng at two ankers men haue tolde,
For if the tone faile, the tother maie holde.
But you leaue all anker holde, on ſeas or lands.
And ſo ſet vp ſhop vpon Goodwins ſands.
But as folke haue a ſaiyng bothe olde and trew,
In that they ſay blacke will take none other hew.
So maie I ſaie here, to my déepe dolour,
It is a bad clothe that will take no colour.
This caſe is yours. For ye were neuer ſo wiſe,
To take ſpecke of colour, of good aduyſe.
Thaduyſe of all fréends I ſay, one and other
Went in at the tone eare, and out at the tother.
And as thoſe woordis went out, this prouerbe in came,
He that will not be ruled by his owne dame,
Shall be ruled by his ſtepdame, and ſo you.
Hauyng loſt your owne good, and owne fréendis now,
Maie ſéeke your forein fréendis, if you haue any.
And ſure one of my great gréefes, among many,
Is that ye haue bene ſo veraie a hog,
To my fréendis. What man, loue me, loue me dog.
But you to caſt precious ſtones before hogs,
Caſt my good before a ſort of cur dogs.
And ſawte bitches. Whiche by whom now deuoured.
And your honeſtie amonge them defloured,
And that you maie no more expence a foorde,
Now can they not afoord you one good woorde,
And you them as fewe. And olde folke vnderſtoode,
Whan théeues fall out, true men come to their goode.

                                               Whiche

Whiche is not alwaie true. For in all that bretche,
I can no ferthing of my good the more fetche.
Nor I trow them felues neither, if thei were fworne,
Light come, light go. And fure fens we were borne,
Ruine of one rauine, was there none gretter.
For by your giftes, they be as littell the better.
As you be muche the woorfe and I caft awaie.
An yll wynde that blowth no man to good, men fay.
Well (quoth he) euery wind blowth not downe the corne.
I hope (I faie) good happe be not all out worne.
I will nowe begin thrift, whan thrift femeth gone.
What wife there be mo waies to the wood than one.
And I will affaie all the waies to the wood,
Till I fynde one waie, to get againe this good.
Ye will get it againe (quoth fhe) I feare,
As fhortly as a horfe will licke his eare.
The Ducheman faieth, that feggyng is good cope.
Good woordes bryng not euer of good déedes good hope,
And thefe woordis fhew your woordis fpoken in fkorne.
It pricketh betymes that will be a good thorne.
Timely crooketh the trée, that will a good camok bée.
And fuch beginnyng fuch ende. we all daie fée.
And you by me at begynnyng beyng thryuen,
And than to kéepe thrift could not be prickt nor driuen.
How can ye now get thrift, the ftocke beyng gone?
Which is thonely thing to reife thrift vpon.
Men faie he maie yll renne, that can not go,
And your gain, without your ftocke, renneth euen fo.
For what is a woorkman, without his tooles?
Tales of Robin hood are good among fooles.
He can yll pype, that lackth his vpper lyp.
Who lackth a ftocke, his gaine is not woorth a chip,
A tale of a tub, your tale no truth auouth,
Ye fpeake now, as ye would créepe into my mouth,

K iij

In

77

In pure peinted proceffe, as falfe as fayre.
How ye will amend, whan ye can not apayre.
But againft gaie glofers, this rude text recites,
It is not all butter, that the coow fhites.
I herd ones a wife man faie to his daughter,
Better is the laft fmyle, than the fyrft laughter,
We fhall I truft (quoth he) laugh againe at laft.
Although I be ones out of the faddle caft.
Yet fens I am bent to fyt, this will I doo,
Recouer the hors, or léefe the faddle too.
Ye neuer could yet (quoth fhe) recouer any hap,
To win or faue ought, to ftop any one gap.
For ftoppyng of gaps (quoth he) care not a rufhe,
I will learne, to ftop two gaps with one bufhe.
Ye will (quoth fhe) as foone ftop gaps with rufhes,
As with any hufbandly handfome bufhes,
Your tales haue lyke taft, where temprance is tafter,
To breake my heade, and than geue me a plafter.
Now thrifte is gone, now would ye thryue in all hafte.
And whan ye had thrift, ye had like hafte to wafte.
Ye liked then better an ynche of your wyll,
Than an ell of your thrift. Wife (quoth he) be ftill.
Maie I be holpe foorth an ynche at a pinche,
I will yet thriue (I faie) As good is an inche
As an ell. Ye can (quoth fhe) make it fo, well.
For whan I gaue you an ynche, ye tooke an ell.
Till both ell and inche be gone, and we in det.
Naie (quoth he) with a wet fynger ye can fet,
As muche as maie eafyly all this matter eafe,
And this debate alfo pleafantly appeafe.
I could doo as muche with an hundred pround now,
As with a thoufand afore, I affure yow.
Ye (quoth fhe) who had that he hath not, woulde
Doo that he dooth not, as olde men haue tolde.

Had

Had I, as ye haue, I woulde dooe more (quoth hée)
Than the préeſt ſpake of on ſonday, ye ſhould ſée.
Ye dooe, as I haue (quoth ſhe) for nought I haue,
And nought ye dooe. What man, I trow ye raue,
Wolde ye bothe eate your cake, and haue your cake?
Ye haue had of me all that I might make.
And be a man neuer ſo greedy to wyn,
He can haue no more of the foxe but the ſkyn.
Well (quoth he) if ye liſt to bring it out,
Ye can geue me your bleſſyng in a clout.
That were for my child, (quoth ſhe) had I ony,
But huſband, I haue neither child, nor mony.
Ye caſt and coniecture this muche like in ſhow,
As the blind man caſts his ſtaffe, or ſhootes the crow.
How be it had I money right muche, and ye none,
Yet to be plaine, ye ſhulde haue none, for Ione.
Nay, he that firſt flattereth me, as ye haue doone.
And doth as ye did to me after, ſo ſoone.
He maie be in my Pater noſter in déede.
But be ſure, he ſhall neuer come in my Créede.
Aue Maria (quoth he) how much mocion
Here is to praiers, with how littell deuocion.
But ſome men ſaie, no peny no Pater noſter.
I ſaie to ſuche (ſaid ſhe) no longer ſoſter,
No longer lemman. But faire and well than,
Praie and ſhifte eche one for him ſelfe, as he can.
Euery man for him ſelfe, and god for us all.
To thoſe woordis he ſaide nought, but foorthwith did fall,
From harping on that ſtringe, to faire flattring ſpéeche,
And as I erſt ſaide, he did hir ſo beſéeche,
That thingis erſt ſo far of, were now ſo far on,
That as ſhe maie wallow, awaie ſhe is gon,
Where all that was left laie with a truſtie fréende.
Dwellyng a good walke from hir at the townes eende,

And

And backe again ftreight a haltyng pace fhe hobles.
Bringyng a bag of royals and nobles.
All that fhe had, without reftraint of one iote,
She brought bullockis noble. for noble or grote,
Had fhe not one mo. Whiche I after well knew.
And anon fmiling, toward him as fhe drew,
A fir light burdeine far heauy (quoth fhe)
This light burdein in longe walke welny tryeth me.
God geue grace I play not the foole this daie.
For here I fende thaxe after the helue awaie.
But if ye will ftint and auoyd all ftryfe,
Loue and cherifhe this as ye wolde my lyfe,
I will (quoth he) wife, by god almightie.
This geare comth euen in puddyng time rightlie.
He fnacht at the bag. No haft but good (quoth fhe)
Short fhootyng léefeth your game, ye maie fée.
Ye myft the cufhin, for all your haft to it.
And I may fet you befyde the cufhyn yit.
And make you wype your nofe vpon your fléeue,
For ought ye fhall win without ye axe me léeue.
Haue ye not heard tell all couet all léefe:
A fir, I fée, ye may fée no gréene chéefe
But your téeth muft water. A good cocknay coke.
Though ye loue not to bye the pyg in the poke,
Yet fnatche ye at the poke, that the pyg is in,
Not for the poke, but the pyg good chepe to wyn.
Like one halfe loft, till gredy grafpyng gat it,
Ye would be ouer the ftyle, er ye come at it.
But abyde freend, your mother bid till ye were borne.
Snatching winth it not, if ye fnatche tyll to morne.
Men faie (faid he) long ftandyng and fmall offring
Maketh poore perfons. and in fuche fignes and proffring.
Many prety tales, and mery toies had they,
Before this bag came fully from hir awey.

                                            Kindly

Kindly he kyſt hir, with woords not tart nor tough.
But the cat knoweth whoſe lips ſhe lickth well enough.
Anone, the bag ſhe deliuered him, and ſaide,
He ſhould beare it, for that it now heauy waide.
With good will wife, for it is (ſaid he to her)
A proude horſe that will not beare his own prouander.
And oft before ſéemd ſhe neuer ſo wyſe,
Yet was ſhe nowe, ſodeinly waxen as nyſe
As it had bene a halporth of ſyluer ſpoones,
Thus cloudy mornynges turne to cléere after noones.
But ſo ny noone it was, that by and by,
They roſe, and went to diner louyngly.

The. x. chapiter.

THis diner thought he long. and ſtreight after that,
To his accuſtomed cuſtomers he gat.
With whom in what tyme he ſpent one grote before,
In leſſe time he ſpenth now, ten grotes or more
And in ſmall tyme he brought the world ſo about,
That he brought the bottome of the bag cleane out.
His gaddyng thus againe made hir ill content.
But ſhe not ſo much as dreamd that all was ſpent,
How be it ſodeinly ſhe mynded on a daie,
To picke the cheſte locke, wherin this bag laie,
Determinyng this, if it laie whole ſtill,
So ſhall it lie, no mite ſhe miniſhe will.
And if the bag began to ſhrinke, ſhe thought beſt,
To take for hir parte ſome parte of the reſt.
But ſtreight as ſhe had foorthwith opened the locke,
And lookt in the bag, what it was a clocke,
Than was it proued trew, as this prouerbe goth,
He that commeth laſt to the pot, is ſooneſt wroth.
By hir commyng laſte, and to late to the pot.
Wherby ſhe was potted, thus lyke a ſot,

L   To

To ſée the pot both ſkymd for rennyng ouer,
And alſo all the licour renne at rouer.
At hir good huſbandes and hir next méetyng,
The diuels good grace might haue geuen a gréetyng.
Eyther for honour or honeſtie as good
As ſhe gaue him. She was (as they ſay) horne wood.
In no place could ſhe ſit hir ſelfe to ſettle,
It ſéemd to him, ſhe had piſt on a nettle.
She nettled him, and he rattled hir ſo,
That at ende of that fraie, aſunder they go.
And neuer after came together againe.
He turnde hir out at doores to graſe on the playne.
And him ſelfe went after. For within fortnight,
All that was left, was launched out quyght.
And thus had he brought haddocke to paddocke.
Till they both were not woorth a haddocke.
It hath bene ſaied, néede maketh the olde wife trot.
Other folke ſaide it, but ſhe did it God wot.
Firſt from fréend to fréend, and than from dur to dur.
A beggyng of ſome that had begged of hur.
But as men ſaie, miſery maie be mother,
Where one begger is dryuen to beg of an other.
And thus ware, and waſted this moſt wofull wretche.
Tyll death from this lyfe, did hir wretchedly fetche.
Her late huſbande, and now wydower, here and there
Wandryng about few know, and fewer care where.
Caſte out as an abiect, he leadeth his lyfe,
Tyll famine by lyke, fet him after his wyfe.
    Now let vs note here, Fyrſt of the fyrſt twayne,
Where they both wedded together, to remayne,
Hopyng ioyfull preſence ſhuld weare out all wo.
Yet pouertée brought that ioye to ioefaile, lo.
But notably note theſe laſt twayne, where as hée
Tooke hir onely, for that he riche wolde bée.

                                              And

And she him onely in hope of good happe,
In hir dotyng daies to be daunst on the lappe.
In condicion thei differde so many waies,
That lightly he layde hir vp for hollie daies.
Hir good he layd vp so, leste théeues might spie it.
That nother she could, nor he can come by it.
Thus failed all foure, of all thinges lesse and more,
Whiche they all, or any of all, maryed fore.

The. xi. chapiter.

Forsooth said my fréend this matter maketh bost,
Of diminucion. For here is a myll post
Thwytten to a puddyng pricke so néerely,
That I confesse me discouraged cléerely.
In both my weddynges, in all thinges, except one.
This sparke of hope haue I, to procede vpone.
Though these and some other, spede yll as ye tell,
Yet other haue lyued and loued full well.
If I should deny that (quoth I) I should raue.
For of both these sorts, I graunt, that my selfe haue,
Séene of the tone forte, and hard of the tother,
That lyked and lyued right well, eche with other.
But whether fortune will you, that man declare,
That shall choose in this choice, your comfort or care,
Sens, before ye haue chosen, we can not know,
I thought to laie the woorst, as ye the best show.
That ye might, beyng yet at libertie,
With all your ioye, ioygne all your ieoperdie.
And nowe in this herde, in these cases on eche parte,
I say no more, but lay your hand on your harte.
 I hartily thanke you (quoth he) I am sped
Of mine errande. This hitteth the nayle on the hed.
Who that leaueth surety and leaneth vnto chaunce,
Whan fooles pype, by auctoritée he maie daunce.

L ij

And

83

And fure am I, of thofe twayne, if I none choofe,
Although I nought wyn, yet fhall I nought loofe.
And to wyn a woman here, and lofe a man,
In all this great winnyng, what gain win I than?
But marke how foly hath me away caryed.
How like a wethercocke I haue here varyed.
Firft thefe two women to loofe, I was fo lothe,
That if I might, I woulde haue wedded them bothe
Than thought I fens, to haue wedded one of them.
And now know I cléere, I will wed none of them.
They both fhall haue this one aunfwere by letter,
As good neuer a whit as neuer the better.
  Nowe let me axe (quoth I) and your felfe anfwere,
The fhort queftion, that I afked while ere.
A foule olde riche widowe, whether wed would ye,
Or a yonge fayre mayde, beyng poore as ye be.
In neither barrell better hearyng (quoth hee)
I lyke thus, richeffe as yll as pouertée.
Who that hath either of thefe pygs in vre,
He hath a pyg of the woorfe panier fure.
I was wedded vnto my wyll. How be it,
I will be deuorft, and be wed to my wyt.
Wherby with thefe examples pafte, I maie fée,
Fonde weddyng, for loue, as good onely to flée.
Onely for loue, or onely for good,
Or onely for both I wed not, by my hood.
Thus no one thing onely, though one thing chiefly
Shall woo me to wed now: for now I efpy,
Although the chiefe one thing in wedding be loue,
Yet muft mo things ioygne, as all in one maie moue.
Suche kynde of lyuyng, for fuche kynde of lyfe,
As lackyng the fame, no lacke to lacke a wife.
Here is enough, I am fatiffied (faid he.)
Sens enough is enough (faid I) here maie we,

With

84

With that one woord take ende good, as may be geaft.
For falke faie, enough is as good as a feaft.

FINIS.

The firste hundred of Epigrammes.
Inuented and
made
by
John Hey=
wood.

LONDINI
1562.

To the reader.

Yme without reafon, and reafon without ryme,
In this conuercion deepe diffrence doth fall.
In firft part wherof where I am falne this time.
The foly I graunte, which graunted (readers all)
Your graunt, to graunt this requeft, require I fhall,
Ere ye full reiecte thefe trifles folowyng here
Perceiue (I praie you) of the woordes thentents clere.

¶In whiche (maie ye like to looke) ye fhall efpie
Some woordes, fhewe one fence, a nother to difclofe,
Some woordes, them felfes fondrie fenfes fignifie:
Some woordes, fomewhat from common fence, I difpofe,
To feeme one fence in text, a nother in glofe.
Thefe words in this work, thus wrought your working toole
Maie woorke me to feeme (at leaft) the les a foole.

¶Than in rough rude termes of homelie honeftie
(For vnhoneft terme (I truft) there none here foundes)
Wherin fine tender eares fhal offended bee
Thofe folies, beyng fercht in reafons boundes.
Reafon maie bee furgion faluyng thofe woundes.
Turning thofe fores to falues: for reafon doth geffe
Homely matters, homly termes dooe beft expreffe.

¶But where all defence ftandth in exempcion
To defend me herein out of folies bandes.
So that to redeme me thers no redempcion.
Graunting, and fubmitting foly, that fo ftandes.
This laft refuge I craue to haue, at your handes,
Thofe folies ftanding cleere from intent of yll.
In lieu or lacke of good wit, except good will.

The table to this booke.

Biyng

Finis Tabulæ.

The fyrſt hundred of Epigrammes.

THis booke maie ſéeme, as it ſorteth in ſute,
 A thyn trym trencher to ſerue folke at frute.
But caruer or reader can no waie win,
To eate frute theron, or compt frute therin.

   Of three ſages.   2.
 Thrée maner ſages nature dooth deuiſe,
The ſage herbe, the ſage foole, and the ſage wiſe.
And who for moſte wyſe him ſelfe dooth accept,
Maie matche any ſage, the ſage wiſe except.

   Queſtions anſwered.   3.
Truſt thei any,   } ye.
That truſt not many ? }

Pleaſe they any,   } Nay.
That ſerue many ? }

Helpe they any,   } ye.
That helpe not many? }

Fréende they any, } Nay.
That flatter many ? }

Feare they any,   } ye.
That feare not many ? }

Kéepe they any,   } Nay.
That kéepe to many? }

   Of water, wine, and ale.   4.
 Water vnder a bote, wine in a bottell,
The tone I can beare, thother bearth me well,

     M   And

89

And where as nother botes nor bottels bée,
Nother can I beare wyne, nor water beare mée.
But aboue all licour welfare ale (I ſaie)
For I with ale, and ale with me wag away.

To muche or to little. 5.

If that I drinke to muche, than am I drie,
If I drinke to littell, more drie am I:
If I drinke no whit than am I dryeſt.
To muche, to little, no whit, nought is the beſt,
Thus drinke we no whit, or drinke tyll we burſt,
Yet poore drie ſoules we be euer a thurſt.

Of the ſenſes. 6.

Speake not to muche, leſt ſpéeche make the ſpéecheleſſe,
Go not to muche, for feare thou go behynde,
Here not to muche, leſt hearyng bring deafneſſe.
Looke not to muche, leſt lookyng make the blynde.
Smell not to muche, leſt ſmellyng loſe his kynde.
Taſt not to muche, leſte taſte miſtaſt thy chaps.
Touche not to muche for feare of after claps.

Of talkyng. 7.

Thy tayle can talke, and knowth no letter,
Thy tounge can talke and talkth much ſwetter.
But except wiſdome be the gretter,
Of tounge and tayle, thy tayle talkth better.

Of heares and wyttes. 8.

Thinne heares and thicke wittes be deyntée,
Thicke heares and thicke wittes be pleintée.
Thicke heares and thicke wittes be ſkant,
Thinne heares and thinne wittes none want.

A dronkard. 9.

A gooſe is harneſt in hir white fethers,
A drunkard in drynke againſt all weathers.
A foole in his fooles hood, put all togethers.

The

The foxe and the mayde. 10.

Although that foxes haue bene ſeene there ſeelde,
Yet was there lately in Fynſbery feelde
A foxe ſate in ſyght of certayne people,
Noddyng, and blyſſyng, ſtaryng on poules ſteeple.
A maide toward market with hens in a band
Came by, and with the fox ſhe fell in hand.

What thing is it Rainard in your brain ploddyng,
That bringeth this buſy bliſſing and noddyng?
I nother nod for ſleepe ſweete herte the foxe ſayde,
Nor bliſſe for ſpirites, excepte the diuell be a mayde.
My noddyng and blyſſyng breedth of wonder,
Of the witte of Poules wethercocke yonder.
There is more witte in that cocks onely head,
Than hath bene in all mens heades that be deade.
As thus, by common reporte this we fynde,
All that be dead, did die for lacke of wynde.
But the wethercocks witte is not ſo weake
To lacke wynde: the wynde is euer in his beake.
So that while any wynde blowth in the ſkie,
For lacke of winde that wethercocke will not die.

She caſt downe hir hennes, and now did ſhe blis,
Ieſu (quoth ſhe) *in nomine patris,*
Who hath euer heard at any ſeaſon
Of a foxes forgeyng ſo feat a reaſon?
And while ſhe preyſed the foxes wyt ſo,
He gat hir hens in his necke and to go.

Whither awaie with my hens foxe (quoth ſhe?)
To poules pig as faſt as I can (quoth he)
Betwene theſe hennes, and yonder wethercock
I will aſſaie to haue chickens a flock.
Whiche if I may get, this tale is made goode,
In all Chriſtendome not ſo wiſe a broode.

M ij   Maiden

Maidén (quoth he) theſe hens be forbodden
Your ſight, tyll the wethercock hath trodden.
Wo woorth (quoth ſhe) all craftie inuencions,
And all inuenters, that by fals intencions,
Inuent with intent to blynd or bleare blunt eies,
In caſe as this fox to me doeth deuiſe.

Of an yll gouernour called Iude.   11.

A ruler there was in countrey a fer,
And of the people a great extorcioner:
Who by name (as I vndeſtand) was called Iude,
One gaue him an aſſe, whiche gyft when he had veude,
He aſked the geuer, for what intent
He brought him that aſſe. For a preſent
I bryng maiſter Iude (quoth he) this as hyther,
To ioygne maiſter Iude and this as together.
Whiche two ioygned in one, this is brought to pas,
I maie byd you good euen maiſter Iudas.
Macabe or Iſcariot thou knaue (quoth he?)
Whom it pleaſe your maſterſhip, him let it be.

Of geuyng an almes.   12.

Into a beggars hande, that almes did craue,
In ſtéede of one peny, two penſe one gaue.
Whiche doone, he ſaide beggar happie thou art,
For to the my hand is better then my hart.
That is (quoth the begger) as it chaunceth now,
The better for me, and the woorſe for yow.

Of a ſurfet.   13.

¶A man from a feuer recouered new,
His gréedy appetite could not eſchew,
From meate contagious, wherto he had a luſt,
But one morſell one euening, nedes eate he muſt.
Whiche foorthwith brought good approbacion,
Of his retourne into reſidiuacion.

What

What caufe caufeth this (quoth the phificion?)
I know (quoth he) no caufe of fufpicion.
How be it my wonder is great as can be,
By what meane this feuer attacheth me
More, for eatyng a littell this night laft,
Than for eatyng muche more the night before paft.
I did eate a capon nie euery whit
The laft night: after whiche, I felt no fit.
And this night I éete but one bit of frefh béefe.
And yet I am fhaken with the hourfon théefe.
   Now (quoth the phificion) apéerth the caufe why
Capon is holfome, and the béefe contrary.
And a littell yll meate geueth ficknefse more foode,
Than a littell to muche of meate that is goode.
   Sir, I thanke you muche (quoth the pacient)
This leffon fhall henffoorth make me to confent,
Whan I fhall néedes furfet, by vnruly will,
Rather to furfet on that is good, than yll.

Repugnancie in apparance. 14.

   Muche contrarietée may féeme to ftand
Where none is. as by example, my fon.
In London is the beft ale of all England:
And yet as good ale in England as in London.

The ape and the affe. 15.

   The ape and the affe ftoode, where they behéelde.
A courfe with a greyhound at the hare in a féelde.
They well perceiuyng, the greyhound great ground wan.
As long as the hare and he foorthright ran.
And like aduauntage they fawe in the hare,
Whan fhe lift lightly to turne here and thare.
The ape to know whether the affis talkyng,
Were any quicker than his affhis ftalkyng.
Afked the affe: if thou fhouldeft choofe one of bothe,
To ren as fwiftly as the greyhound yonder gothe

Or turne as light as the hare: whiche one of twaine
Wouldſt thou in thy chooſyng by choyſe obtaine?
   I (quoth the aſſe) beyng at lybertée,
Will chooſe none of bothe feates, I may ſay to thée.
What winneth the dog by his ſwift footemanſhip?
When the hare at pinche turnth from him at a whip.
And what winth the hare in hir turns ſo lightly,
The dog out rennyng hir againe by and by?
Rennyng or turnyng ſo, ren or tourne who will,
I will goe ſoftly, or els ſtand euen ſtill.
Howbete to aſſoyle thy queſtion (quoth he)
If I ſhould chooſe one, lyke the hare would I be.
For where the dog renneth the hare for to kyll,
She turnth for defence, offring the dog none yll.
And better is this part in this caſe brother,
My ſelfe to defend, then offend an other.

A foole and a wiſe man.   16.

   A foole and a wyſe man ridyng one eſpyde.
He aſked the horſe, that the wyſe man dyd ryde,
Whither goſte thou horſe? whither go I (quoth he?)
Aſke him that guideth the brydell, aſke not me.
Whither rydeſt thou foole (quoth he) with looke ſo fell?
Aſke my horſe knaue (ſaid he) what can I tell.
Whan fooles ryde (quoth he) that can not rule the raine
Their horſes be their herbengers, I ſée plaine.
And when wiſe men ryde, I right well eſpie,
Them ſelfe, not their horſe, apointe where they lie.

Of ſyght.   17.

   Who néedes will looke, and would not ſée,
The ſyght once ſéene thou lookeſt fore,
Cloſe vp thine eies. For truſt thou me.
Muche lookyng ſo, bréedth much eie fore.

Feigned

Feigned newes.   18.

From a féeld fought, one of the beaten fyde,
Ran home, and victorie on his part he cride.
Whofe prince by him thus enfourmed of this,
Made bonfiers and bankettes, as the vfe is.
In fhort tyme after all whiche ioie and coft,
The kynge was acertaind, the féeld was loft.
Wherwith he (in as great haft as great gréefe)
Charged the fyrft meffenger to make préefe,
Where he had this lie, that the féeld was wonne.
My felfe fir (quoth he) this lie fyrft begonne.
Which for commoditée vnto your grace
And all your fubiectes, I brought it in place.
Where the truth fhould haue brought watchyng and wéeping,
My lie brought two daies of laughyng and fléeping.
And if ye all this yere tooke my lye for true,
To kepe you mery, what harme could enfue?
Better is (quoth he) be it new or ftale,
A harmeleffe lie, than a harmefull true tale.
How his ly was aloude, I know none that knowth.
But it was at leaft winkt at, I heard of trowth.

Two, arme in arme.   19.

One faid to an nother takyng his arme,
By licence fréend, and take this for none harme.
No fir (quoth the other) I geue you léeue
To hang on my arme, but not on my fléeue.

Of hearyng and fpeakyng.   20.

Who heareth all
And fpeaketh nought,
Chaunce maie fo fall
He is well tought.
Who fpeaketh all
And heareth nought

Fall

Fall what ſhall fall,
He is ill tought.
Who heareth all,
And all bableth,
What euer fall
He ofte fableth.
Who hereth nought,
Nor nought can ſpeake,
Maie ſoone be thought
A hodie peake.
Saie nought, here all,
Saie all, here nought,
Both, none, theſe fall
Extremely wrought.
Who hereth oft,
And ſpeaketh féeld,
Be witte alofte
He wynth the féeld.

Of wit, will, and wiſdome. 21.

Where will is good, and wit is yll,
There wiſdome can no maner ſkyll.
Where wit is good, and will is yll,
There wiſdome ſitteth all ſilent ſtill.
Where wit and will are both two yll,
There wiſdome no waie meddle will,
Where wit and will well ordred bée,
There wiſdome makth a trinitée.

The wrenne, and hir birdes. 22.

Of a neſt of wrens late bred in a hedge,
Whiche the dam forſakyng, when they were fledge,
One ſaide: Alas mother what is the why,
That ye draw from vs vnnaturally?
Child (quoth the dam) I dooe now vnto thée,
As my dam in my youth did vnto me.

Wherby

Wherby I am blamleſſe in that I do,
Sens I do but as I haue bene done to.

   Mother (quoth he) to deale as ye be delt with,
Is not alwaie méete: but this is the pith:
As ye would your dam ſhould haue delt with yow,
So ſhould ye our dam deale with your birdes now.

   Why ſonne (quoth ſhe) thinkſt thou me ſuch a foole?
That my childe ſhall ſet his mother to ſcoole?
Nay adieu (quoth ſhe) and away ſhe is flowne:
This childe for this checke refuſyng for hir owne.
Whiche done, the wren calth his brothers and ſiſters,
And vnto them this leſſon he whiſters.
I ſée and ye may ſée (quoth he) by this caſe,
The triall of tauntes out of tyme and place.
Where faire woordis haply my mother might haue won,
This taunt makth hir refuſe me for hir ſon.
Whiche maie teach vs all, where euer we becum,
Rather by ſilence alway to be mum,
Than in ought at libertée, or forbydden,
To taunt our betters, openly or hydden.

   The maiſter and the man.   23.
   A man, and his man, chaunced late to bée
Nie where a crowe ſtoode criyng in a trée.

   Iames (quoth the maiſter) the crow hath ſpyde thée.
Nay by God, he loketh on you maiſter (quoth he)
Taunts (quoth the maiſter) rebound ſomtyme I ſée.
Where I thought to taunt thée, thou doeſt taunt mée.

   Vpon penance.   24.
   Two men of one man were confeſt but late,
And both two had penaunce after one rate.
Which was : eche of them a peny ſhould geue
To a peniles man, him to releue.
Thone of theſe twayne had one peny and no more.
Thother, no peny nor farthyng had in ſtore.

                         N   They

97

They diſcloſyng eche to other in this caſe.
This peny father drue his purſe apaſe,
Saiyng: ſens thou art penileſſe, I will
Geue the this peny, my penance to fulfill.

God thanke the (quoth the tother) and ſens thow
Art now peniles, as I was euen now,
For penaunce I geue this peny to thée,
As fréely as euer thou gaueſt it to mée.
Well done (quoth the other) here may we boſt,
Peny dole delt, without one peny coſte.

Iacke and his father. 25.

Iacke (quoth his father) how ſhall I eaſe take?
If I ſtand, my legges ake, and if I knéele,
My knées ake, If I goe, then my féete ake,
If I lie, my backe akthe, If I ſit I féele
My hyps ake : and leane I neuer ſo wéele,
My elbowes ake : Sir (quoth Iacke) peyn to exile,
Sens all theſe eaſe not, beſt ye hang a while.

Of a daw. 26.

With a croſſebowe late in hand readie bent
To ſhoote at a dawe in a trée, I went.
Saiyng to one by : I will aſſaie to hit
Yonder I ſée a daw, if ſhe will ſit.

She is, if ſhe ſit, a daw in déede (quoth he)
But if ſhe ſit not, what is ſhe than ſaie ye?
A daw alſo (ſaid I). Than ſaid he, I ſée,
Whether a daw ſyt, or whether a daw flée,
Whether a daw ſtand, or whether a daw lie,
Whether a daw creke, or whether a daw crie,
In what caſe ſo euer a daw, perſeuer,
A daw is a daw, and a daw ſhall be euer.

Of ſhewyng the waie. 27.

Twaine met in a high waie, what tyme they did go,
Eche one toward the place the tother came fro.

What

What is my waie (faide the tone) I pray the?
Foule (quoth thother.) That is yll tidynges (quoth he.)
I can tell the better tidyngis then this:
Thy way, both faire and fmooth as a dye is.
My tidynges (quoth he) is better then thyne,
But I thinke thy tidyngis truer then mine.
This is (quoth the tother) fo well brought about,
That it brought and fhall bryng me in dout,
Whiche of thefe twayne is moft ill to vew,
Good tales that be falfe, or yll tales that be trew.

    A quiet neighbour.   28.
    Accompted our commoditées,
Few more commodious reafon fées,
Than is this one commoditée,
Quietly neighboured to bée.
Whiche neighbourhood in the apéers.
For we two hauyng ten whole yéers
Dwelt wall to wall, fo ioygninglie,
That whifpering foundeth through welny.
I neuer herd thy feruauntis brall
More than thou hadft had none at all.
Nor I can no way make auaunt,
That euer I heard the geue them taunt.
Thou art to them and they to thée
More milde then muet, mum ye bée.
I heare no noife mine eafe to breake,
Thy buttry doore I here not creake.
The kitchin cumbreth not by heate,
Thy cookes choppe neither herbes nor meate.
I neuer heard thy fyre once fparke,·
I neuer heard thy dog once barke,
I neuer heard once in thy houfe,
So muche as one péepe of one moufe.
       N ij   I

I neuer herd thy catte once mew.
Thefe preyfes are not fmall nor few.
I beare all water of thy foyle,
Wherof I féele no fylthie foyle,
Saue water, which dooth wafh thy handis,
Wherin there none annoiance ftandis.
Of all thy gueftes fet at thy boorde,
I neuer heard one fpeake one woorde.
I neuer heard them coegh nor hem:
I thinke hence to Ierufalem,
For this neighbourlie quietneffe,
Thou art the neighbour neighbourleffe.
For er thou wouldeft neighbours annoy,
Thefe kyndes of quyet to deftroy,
Thou rather wouldeft to helpe that matter,
At home alone faft bread and water.

Of dogges and theeues.   29.

To kepe théeues by night out of my houfe,
I kepe doggis to ayde me in my yarde,
Whofe barkyng at ftur of euery moufe,
By lacke of fléepe kylth me in regarde,
Théeues or dogs than, whiche maie beft be fparde?
Murder is the moft mifchiefe here to geffe,
Théeues can do no more, and dogs will do no leffe.

A keper of the commaundementes.   30.

If it be (as it is) muche commendable,
To kepe Gods preceptes. geuen Moyfes in table:
In kepyng the fame (as thou haft pretended)
Thou maift well be marueyloufly commended.
Firft for thy hauyng any mo gods but one,
Thou kepeft within that bound, For God thou haft none.
Hauyng or woorfhippyng of god falfe or true,
Thou haft nor worfhippeft God olde nor newe.

And

And as for the committyng of Idolatrie,
By grauyng to thy felfe any Imagerie,
This twenty yeres daie in weather hot or coole,
Thou handledft no caruyng nor woorkyng toole.
　　The name of God in vayne thou confentft not till,
Thou neuer fwerft but for fome purpofe good or yll,
　　And as for the holy daie, thou doeft breake none,
For thou wilt rather make twentie then breake one.
　　Father and mother not difhonoured by thée:
For thou neuer comft where any of them bée.
　　And where thou fhalt not kyll, to cléere the of that,
Thou neuer durft abyde to fyght with a gnat.
　　Than all adultery or fornicacion
Chaftitée difchargeth, by this approbacion.
All women hardly can beare the their fauour,
To abyde thy fight: and in no wyfe thy fauour.
　　For ftealyng or theft, what euer thou haft béene,
Thy handes at this daie are knowen to be cléene.
How canft thou fteale ought in houfe, féeld, or ftréete?
Thou fitteft in Newgate faft bound handis and féete.
　　By falfe witneffe thou neuer hurteft man, for why,
Eury woord thou fpeakeft, eury man thinkth a lie.
　　Now, to couet in mynde thy neighbours affe,
Or his houfe, when bondage will not let the paffe.
To ride to the tone, or go to the tother,
Or in confented thought one waie or other.
For to couet thy neighbours maide or his wyfe,
Thou knowyng, they can not loue thée for their lyfe,
Or of thy neighbours thinges to couet any thyng,
Whan couetoufnes can no way bryng winnyng,
But that lacke of credite, libertée, or loue,
Kepth the from that couetyng can moue.
Thou haft to fhrewde a wit in defyre to dwell,
To haue thingis, from whiche difpeyre doth the expell.
　　　　　　N iij　　　　　　　　　　Thus

Thus in gods precepts, except thou cléere appéere,
I know not who the diuell can ſay he is cléere.

Of a noſe.   31.

But for blemiſhe of a face to looke vpon,
I doubt which were beſt, to haue a noſe or none.
Moſt of our ſauours are more ſowre than ſwéete,
A noſe or no noſe, whiche is now moſt méete?

Lettyng of a ferme.   32.

By woord without wrytyng one let out a farme,
The couenaunts wherin the leſſée brake a mayne:
Wherby the leſſor, lackyng wrytyng, had harme.
He ſaide and ſware, he would make promiſe plaine,
Without wrytyng, neuer to let thyng againe.
Huſband cryde this wyfe, that othe agayne reuarte,
Els without wrytyng, ye can not let a farte.

Age and youth.   33.

Though age and youth together can ſéeld agrée,
Yet once two yong and two olde folke did I ſée,
Agréede lyke lams together dyuers yeres.
The ſtorie wherof foorthwith aperes.
A woman olde, and a man young were led,
She him for loue, and he hir for good to wed.
A yong woman, and olde man in lyke caſe,
Were wed for lyke cauſe at the ſame tyme and place.
Into one houſe theſe two couples wedded were,
And duryng their lyues, together muſt liue there.
And they once acquainted, and one month maryed,
All their liues after they neuer varyed.
Company and condicion theſe foure folke hold,
As nature naturally wylth yong and old:
Couplyng them ſelues to gether thus euery daie,
Tholde fooles aldaie prate, the yong fooles aldaie plaie.

A

A rofe and a nettill.   34.

What tyme herbes and wéedes, and fuch thingis could talke,
A man in his gardeine one daie did walke,
Spiyng a nettill gréene (as Themeraude) fpred
In a bed of rofes lyke the rubie red.
Betwene whiche two colours, he thought by his eye,
The gréene nettill did the red rofe beautifie.
How be it he afked the nettill, what thing
Made him fo pert ? fo nye the rofe to fpringe.
I grow here with thefe rofes, faide the nettill:
Their milde propertées in me to fettill.
And you, in laiyng vnto me your nofe,
Shall fmell, how a nettle maie change to a rofe.
He did fo, whiche done, his noftrils fo pritcht,
That raffhely he rubd, where it no whit itcht,
To whiche fmart mocke, and wyly begylyng,
He the fame fmellyng, faide fmoothly fmylyng,
Rofes conuert nettils ? Nay, they be to fell,
Nettils will peruet Rofes rather, I fmell.

Of the wyues and hir hufbandes wafte.   35.

Where am I leaft hufband ? quoth he, in the waft:
Which comth of this, thou art vengeable ftreit lafte.
Where am I biggeft wife ? in the wafte (quoth fhee)
For all is wafte in you, as far as I fee.

An olde wiues boone.   36.

In olde world, when olde wyues bitterly prayde,
One deuoutly as by way of a boone,
Axt vengeance on hir hufband, and to him faide,
Thou wouldft wed a young wyfe er this wéeke were doone
Wer I dead, but thou fhalt wed the diuel as foone.
I can not wed the diuell (quoth he) why (quoth fhe ?)
For I haue wedded his dam before (quoth he)

A talke

A talke of two conies. 37.

In tyme whan dum beaſtes, as well as birdis ſpake,
Two conies their mindes in this mater brake.
Were all conies in ſuch caſe (ſaid the one)
That of two winters weather we muſt chooſe one?
Whiche were beſt choice, froſt neuer, and ſnowe euer?
Or els to chooſe froſt euer, and ſnow neuer.
Froſt (quoth the other) maketh vs luſtie and fat,
And ſnow lameth vs for leane. What (quoth he) for that?
Fortie fat conies be oft kylde in one night,
Whan leane conies with lyfe ſcape away quight.
Ye (quoth the tother) but where ſnow to long lyeth,
Conies by famin well nie euery one dieth.
Better all be fatte, though ſome die as lotts fall,
Than linger in leanneſſe, and therby die all.

A priſoner. 38.

In priſon, a priſoner condemned to die,
And for execucion waityng daylie,
In his handes for woormes lookyng on a daie,
Smilyng to him ſelfe theſe woordes did ſaie:
Sence my foure quarters in foure quarters ſhall ſtand,
Why harme I theſe féely woormes eatyng my hand?
Nought els in this déede doo I, but my ſelfe ſhow,
Enemy to the woorme and fréend to the crow.

Two blinde men. 39.

One blynde man to ſupper an other bad,
Whiche twayne ſittyng at ſuch meate as they had,
Me thinkth (quoth the blind hoſt) this candell burnth dim.
So thinkth me ſir, ſaide the blind gueſt to him.
Wife (ſaide the good man) with ſorow mend this light.
She put out the candell, whiche burned very bright.
And chopt downe emptie candelſticks two or thrée.
So lo: now eate and welcome neighbour (quoth he.)

Debilitée

Debilitee of senses. 40.
Wyfe, my hands for féelyng are oft very yll.
And as thone hand mendth, thother appeyreth ftill.

Ye faie footh (faid fhe) thone hand féelth euermore,
Woorfe the daie prefent, than the daie before.
Thother hand féeleth by oinctmentes excellent,
Better the day before than the daie prefent.
But how dooth your eye fyght? woorfe and woorfe (faid he.)
For woorfe this daie, than yefterdaie, I fée the.
Though you wer blinde (quoth fhe) that fhuld no loue breake,
I would your eies were out, fo you could not fpeake.

Take hearyng to (quoth he) thou makft my eares fuch,
That thou haft made them here enough, and to muche.
And goyng maie go to. For where euer I am,
I go not an ynche from the diuell or his dam.

In feith if thou didft (quoth fhe) yet could I well
Fynde meane, to fynde out a foole by the fmell.
And here may we here and fée, how this tale fytts,
With my good mans goodly lyms, and good witts.

A foolifhe hufbande. 41.
Hufband, two wittes are better then one, clarks faie,
To debate mattiers : whiche féemeth true this waie.
Whan we two contend whats my wit without thyne,
To conuince thy felfe, thy wyt conducth mine.

A wytty wyfe. 42.
Iane (quoth Iames) to one fhort demaund of myne
Anfwere not with a lie, from that mouth of thine,
And take this noble. Which when fhe had tane,
Is thy hufband (quoth he) a cockold Iane?

She ftoode ftill, and to this would no woord fpeake.
From whiche dum dump when he could hir not breake,
He axt his noble againe. Why (quoth fhe)
Made I any lie to thée? Nay (quoth he.)

O   Than

Than walke foole (quoth ſhe) this wager I wyn cléere,
And thou of my counſel neuer the néere.
Gogs foule (ſware he) and flang away amayne,
I will neuer talke with that woman againe.
For as ſhe in ſpéeche can reuile a man,
So can ſhe in ſilence beguile a man.

Handſom handlyng.   43.

Some wonder to ſée thy handlyng of thingis neate,
But it is no wonder as the caſe ſtandis.
The toes of thy féete in handlyng of thingis feate,
Are as hanſom as the fyngers of thy handis.

A ſaiyng of Patche my lord cardinals foole.   44.

Maſter Sexten, a parſon of knowne wit,
As he at my lord Cardinals boord did ſit,
Gredily raught at a goblet of wyne:
Drinke none (ſaid my lord) for that ſore leg of thine.
I warrant your grace (quoth Sexten) I prouide
For my leg : For I drinke on the tother ſide.

Certaine folies.   45.

To caſt faire white ſalte into wiſe mens meate, } *a foly.*
To make them count ſalt ſuger, when they eate,

To beare a man in hand he itcheth in eche parte } *a foly.*
Whan the man féeleth an vniuerſall ſmarte,

To ſpeake alwaies well, and do alwaies ill, } *a foly.*
And tell men thoſe deedes are doone of good wyll,

Thy luſtie limd horſe to leade in thy hand, } *a foly.*
When on thy lame lyms thou canſt ſcantly ſtand,

Of kyks for cage woorke, to builde thy houſe hie, } *a foly.*
And couer it with leade to kepe thy houſe drie,

Of two ſtudentes.   46.

Two ſcolers yonge in the vniuerſitée late.
Kept in thinne diet, after ſcolars rate,
Thone beyng an eater gréedy and greate,
Thother a weake féeder, ſaid at his meate:

Oh

Oh this fmart fmall pittans, and hungrie diet,
Maketh vs to ftudie aptly and quiet.
　　Sure (faid the tother) fmall meales are induction
To thencreafe of ftudie, for deper inftruction,
This diner fhall driue me to ftudie anon,
Where I maie get more meate, whan this is gon.

　　　　A merie woman.　47.
　　There came by chaunce to a good companie.
A lady, a wanton and a merie.
And though euery woord of hir owne fhowde hir light,
Yet no mans woordis els to hir might that recite:
She had all the woordis, fhe babled fo faft,
That they beyng wéery, one faid at the laft:
Madame, ye make my hert lyght as a kyx,
To fée you thus full of your *meretrix.*
　　This tricke thus well tricked in the latine phrafe,
Brought to this tricker nother mufe nor mafe,
She nought perceiuyng, was no whit offended:
Nor hir light behauiour no whit amended,
But ftill hir tounge was clappyng lyke a paten.
Well, faid the faid man, in language of laten,
I neuer tolde woman any faute before,
Nor neuer in laten will tell them faute more.

　　　　A loufe and a flea.　48.
　　A loufe and a flea, fet in a mans necke,
Began eche other to taunt and to checke.
Difputyng at length all extremitées
Of their pleafures, or difcommoditées.
Namely this I heard, and bare away well.
　　If one (quoth the loufe) fcrat within an ell
Of thy tayle : than foorthwith art thou fkippyng,
Lyke iacke of Bedlem in and out whipping.
Halfe an houre after thou darft no where fyt,
To abyde the bytyng of one good byt.
　　　　　　　　　O ij　　　　　　　　And

And whan any man herein ſhall proue me,
His nailes dooe (as a writte dooth) remoue me.
Whiche nayles once remoued from the mans head,
I am ſtreight at féedyng within a here breade.
Where I fed before in my deyntie diot.
    Ye be hardie (quoth the flea) I deny not,
But how many life haue abydden by it?
Whan they would haue doone as fleas dooe, flie it.
With this the man to his necke his hand raught,
The flea ſkypt away, but the louſe he caught.
How now (quoth the flea.) Alas (quoth the louſe)
My head is well ſerued to ſerue for ſowſe:
That thus like a ſowſe head, forſaw not this gréefe,
Tyll feelyng hath put peinfull practiſe in préefe.

Of him that forgot his pater noſter
in latine.   49.

    An olde homely man at ſhrift commaundid
By his Curate his *pater noſter* to bid.
After long ſtudie, he ſaide : Maſter vicker,
By Iys cham a ſhamd, my wyt is no quicker.
Ich ſaid it within littell more then fortnight.
And now, lyke a beaſt, cha forgote it quight.
Fye on age. In youth Ich had euer ſuche wit,
That what ſo euer Ich had to dooe, yit
At ſhrift chad my *pater noſter* euermore,
Whan Iche ſaide it not twiſe in the yere before.

Of him that could not learne his Pater
noſter in Engliſhe.   50.

    A man of the countrey ſhriuen in Lent late,
(Accordyng to thiniuction) his curate
Bad him, the *Pater noſter* in engliſhe ſaie,
Iche can it not maiſter (quoth he) by my faie.
Saie a péece of it (quoth he) though ye the reſt mys,
Ich can not one woord of it (quoth he) by Iis.

                                          And

And yet maſter vickar, by gods ſacrament,
Cha iumbled about it euer ſens laſt lent.
And ſome of it ich had in the clenſyng wéeke,
But now, whan ich ſhould ſay it, all is to ſéeke.
Well (quoth the prieſt) if your wit be ſo far decayde,
Say the *Pater noſter*, ye haue alway ſayde.
 Nay by the Maſſe (ſware he) if you will haue all tolde,
Cha ſo grated on the new, cha forgot tholde.

Of the fiſt and the hart. 51.

 One curſt an others hart for a blowe in a fume,
Curſe not his hart (quoth one by) curſe his fiſt.
His hert (quoth he) to mine eare did not preſume,
But his hart to mine eare did his fiſt aſſiſt.
Sens eche lim muſt frame in feate, as the hart liſt,
Whan the hart willth any lym in any faute to fall.
No man blame any man, to blame the hart for all.

Of this woorde enough. 52.

 A mery man by his maiſter at mete ſet.
Me thinkth (quoth the maiſter) thou canſt no drinke get.
Here is enough, though there be none ſaid hee:
Than art thou not drie. Yes ſo moote I thee,
And faine would drinke. How be thy wordis true than?
Thus : This woord *enough* twoo waies we may ſkan.
Thone much enough, thother littell enough.
And here is littel enough. His maiſter lough,
Callyng in his wife to diſcant vpon this.
How ſaieſt thou wife? our man in this caſe is
Drie, and would drinke, and drinke nothyng nie him.
And yet proueth he drinke enough by him.
Sens he (quoth ſhe) proueth drinke enough in ſtore,
More then enough were waſt. He getth no more.

Of table play. 53.

 Wife, I will no more play at tables with thée:
When wée come to bearyng, thou begyleſt mée,

O iij In

In bearyng of thy men, while thou haſt any,
Eche other caſte thou beareſt a man to many.

The cocke and the hen.   54.

A cocke and his hen perchyng in the night,
The cocke at his houre crode loude as he might,
The hen heuy of ſlepe, praide the cock that he
Would leaue of his crowyng, but it would not be,
The hen ſaw the cock ſticke to his tacklyng,
In hir treble voyce, ſhe fell ſo to cacklyng,
That the cocke praide hir, hir cacklyng to ſeace,
And he of his crowyng would hold his peace,
Nay chorle (quoth ſhe) be ſure, that will I not.
And for thy learnyng hencefoorth marke this knot.
Whan euer thou wouldeſt ſéeme, to ouer crow mée,
Than will I ſurely ouer cakill thée.

Cheepenyng of a face of furre.   55.

Into a ſkinners ſhop, while his wife there wrought,
In haſt ran a gentilman there to eſpie.
A fayre face of fur, which he woulde haue bought.
What fur (quoth ſhe) would your maiſterſhip bie?
Harlots wombs (quoth he) know ye any nie?
Harlots wombs (forſooth) I haue none (quoth ſhe)
But ye ſhall haue knaues ſhankes, méete as can be.

Biyng of ſhowes.   56.

Whan I at the ſhoemakers ſhall ſhoes aſſay,
If they be to littell, they will ſtretche (ſaith he)
If they be to muche, they will ſhrinke ſtreight way:
To long, to ſhort, how narrow or wide they be,
All is one matter as he ſhapth them to me.
For may he once get his ſhooes on my féete,
Without laſt or lingel his woordes make them méete.

A ſuſpicion cleared.   57.

One to his fréende kiendly,
Gaue monicion friendly,

That

That ill was reported
By one that reforted
To him : whom (as they thought)
Entifed him to nought.
   He thanked him, and fayde,
My fréende, be not afraide.
The heryng of that foole
Setth me no whit to fchoole.
I here him, whan he lift.
And folow him whan me lift.

Of fpite.   58.
   If there be any, as I hope there be none,
That would léefe both his eies, to leefe his foe one,
Than feare I, there be many as the world gothe,
That would léefe one eie, to léefe their foes bothe.

Of the letter H.   59.
   H, is worft among letters in the croffe row,
For if thou finde him other in thine elbow,
In thine arme, or leg, in any degrée,
In thy head, or téeth, in thy toe or knée,
Into what place fo euer H, may pike him,
Where euer thou finde ache, thou fhalt not like him.

Ill fliyng of idelneffe.   60.
   If flight from idelneffe may be déemed.
Mayn meane to vertue beyng fled warely :
How maift thou than therby be eftéemed ?
Thou fléeft that vice not meanly nor barely.
But mainely : fcrupuloufly, and fo charely,
That in thée, er idelneffe fhalbe fpied,
Thou wilt yet rather be ill occupied.

A tounge and a clocke.   61.
   Thy tong fhould be a clocke wife, had I gods power,
For than would it ftrike but once in one hower,
                              Yet

Yet it might ren (quoth ſhe) and ſtrike er the time,
And ſhould that clocke haue (as my tong hath) a chime?
I beyng ſexten, might ſet the clocke foorth ſoone,
To ſtrike and chime. xij. twoo houres before noone.

A hearer of a ſermon. 62.

What bringſt thou from the ſermon Iacke? declare that.
Forſooth maiſter (quoth he) your cloke and your hat.
I can thée good thanke Iacke. for thou art yet ſped,
Of ſomwhat in thy hande, though nought in thy hed.

A man without wit, ſtrength, and cunnyng. 63.

Thou art a wight to wonder at.
Thy head, for wit, ſhowth thee a wat.
Thy bodie for ſtrength ſhewth thée a gnat.
Thy voyce for tune ſheweth thée a cat.
Doo, ſay, or ſyng, in any what,
Thou art a minion marmſat.

How to wiſhe. 64.

How may I haue thée Gill, whan I wiſhe for thée?
Wiſhe not for me Iacke, but whan thou maiſt haue mée.
This is a leſſon Gill propre and pleaſaunt.
For by theſe woordes this winning Iacke may auaunt,
Though Iacke be no nere Gill then Iacke was before,
Yet Iack is nere his wit, by gis, by ten ſcore.

A doubtfull demaunde of choiſe. 65.

If thou muſt chooſe Hodge, touchyng cockoldry,
Which wouldſt thou chooſe? to know thy ſelf commonly
To be taken for one : and take thy ſelfe none,
Or to be taken for none, and take thy ſelf one?
The beſt or worſt of theſe twayne (Hew) tel me whiche
Claw wher it doth ſmart, or tikell, where it doth itche?

I know ſmall difference herein, Hodge brother,
And I (Hugh) know as littell in the tother.

An

An olde widower and a yong mayde. 66.

A widower riche, with riueld face old,
Wooyng a fayre yong woman, his minde he told.
Boftyng what he had, as wowers doe, that can,
Wherin he bofted of a goodly yong man.
A fon of his owne, whome god had him fent,
Of condicions and qualitees excellent,
In this whot wooyng this old mans behauour
So far foorth had won this yong womans fauour,
That in fhort tale, whan his long tale was don,
She prayd him to go home, and fend hir his fon.

Gapyng Oyfters. 67.

On whom gape thine Oyfters fo wide, oyfterwife?
Mine Oyfters gape on you fir, god faue your life.
Wherfore gape they? Sir they gape for promocion.
They hope (to promote them) you haue deuocion.
Nay (quoth he) the perill were pernicious,
To promote oyfters, that be ambicious.

The Iudge and the Iuggler. 68.

To a iuftice a iuggler did complaine
Of one, that difpraifed his liger demaine.
Whats thy name (fayd the iuftice) Daufon faid hée.
Is thy father aliue? Nay, dead fir pardée.
Than thou fhalt no more be Daus fon, a clere cafe,
Thou art Daw thy felf now, in thy fathers place.

Of lookyng. 69.

To faue mine head, whan I vpward caft mine eie,
And looke not to my féete : to the ground fall I,
Whan I looke downeward to my féete, to take héede,
A tile falne from a houfe makth my hed bléede.
And looke I right foorth, betwéene my féete and hed,
Broken head, breke necke falls, of both I am fped.
I thinke it as good, by ought I can deuife,
To be ftarke ftaryng blinde, as thus to haue eies.

P   *Of*

Of conſtancie. 70.

Some ſay, thou art inconſtant, but I ſay nay,
What though thy wit be wauryng euery way?
Whoſe wit like the winde hath been wauryng euer,
And in vnſtedy wauryng doth perſeuer,
A conſtant man I affirme him conſtantly,
For he is conſtant in inconſtancy.

Of a face and a witte. 71.

In thy youth and age theſe properties are ſprong,
In youth thy face was olde, in age thy wit is yong.

Of blowyng. 72.

What winde can there blow, that doth not ſome man pleaſe?
A fart in the blowyng doth the blower eaſe.

To the flatterer. 73.

Thy flatteryng of me, this foloweth thervpon.
Other thou art a foole, or els I am one.
Where flattrie aperth, at leaſt, by wyſe mens ſchoole
The flattrer, or the flattred, is a foole.

Of contentacion. 74.

Is not the poore man riche, that is contented?
Yes: riche by his contentacion conſented.
Is not the riche man poore, that is not content?
Yes: poore by lacke of contentacion here ment.
Than riches and pouertee in mens mindes lie.
Ye: but we may far ſooner learne (thinke I)
To thinke our ſelues riche, hauyng no riches nie,
Than make our ſelues riche, hauyng much riches by.

Of waytyng. 75.

I would ſee a man waite to his maiſters minde,
As the weathercock waiteth on the winde,
Blow it here or there, blow it low or hie,
The weathercockis beke is ſtill in the windis eie.

Of fore knowlage. 76.

Foreknowlage of thingis that muſt fall

To

To man, I thinke it were not beſt.
The fore knowne ill to man, would call
Fore felt gréefe, of fore knowne vnreſt.
By foreknowen good to man were feſt
Swéete fodain ioy, which euermore
Comth, whan ioyes come vnknowne before.

The ſame impungned without chaunge of
wordes, except foure or fiue.

Foreknowlage of thinges that muſt fall
To man, I thinke it were the beſt,
The fore knowen il to man, would call
Digeſtion, of fore knowen vnreſt,
By fore knowen good to man, were feſt
Diſtemperate ioy, whiche euermore
Comth, whan ioyes come vnknowne before.

Miſtakyng an errand. 77.

Feaſtyng a freend, the feaſter (whoſe man did waite)
Bad him at the laſt courſe, fetche the clouted conceite.
What bringſt thou here knaue (quoth he) what haſt ẙ doone?
I haue (quoth his man) brought here your clouted ſhoone.
Clouted ſhoone carterly knaue, what doſt thou dreame?
Eate thou the clouted ſhoone, fetche vs the clouted creame.

Of holdyng an Inne. 78.

Beyng holden in Newgate, thou canſt not bée
An inholder, for thine Inne holdeth thée.

A wiues defence of hir beetill
brow. 79.

Were I to wed againe wife, I make a vow,
I would not wed a wife with a beetill brow.

And I (quoth ſhe) rather would a huſband wed
With a béetill brow, than with a béetell hed.

The ſhrewde wiues tounge. 80.

A dog dame ruleth in degree
Aboue a diuell with thee:

P ij   At

115

At left ſower winde a dog letth flée,
Thy noſe will ſtopped bee:
But no deuils word may make decree
To ſtoppe thy toung I ſee,
　Sens thou aperſt to be (quoth ſhe)
A dogged deuill to mee,
To tame thy deuilliſh propertee,
My tounge ſhall ſtill be free.

A fooles tounge.　81.

Vpon a fooles prouocacion
A wiſe man will not talke:
But euery light inſtigacion
May make a fooles toung walke.

Of glas and lattiſe.　82.
Where glaſiers and lattiſe makers worke in ſight,
This one difference in their twoo feates wée finde:
Glas kéepeth out the winde and letth in the light,
Lattiſe kéepeth out the light and letth in the winde.
Of both ſortis I wiſhe, whan I ſhall wiſh any,
Lattiſe makers few, and glaſiers many.

Two wiſſhers for two maner of
mouthes.　83.

I wiſſhe thou hadſt a littell narrow mouth wife,
Littell and littell to droppe out wordis in ſtrife.
And I wiſſhe you ſir, a wide mouth for the nonce,
To ſpeake all that euer you ſhall ſpeake at once.

Of diſpraiſe.　84.
All men muſt be blinde and deafe er thou prayſe win.
For no man ſeeth or herth ought to prayſe thée in.

A diſcharge from hipocriſie.　85.
Thou art no birde of hipocriſie broode.
For thou fléeſt all thingis, that might ſhew thée goode.

Of

116

Of the foole and the gentlemans
nofe. 87.

One gentilman hauyng an other at meate,
That gueft hauyng a nofe deformd foule and great.
The foole of that houfe, at this tyme ftandyng by,
Fell thus in hand with that nofe fodeinly.
   Nofe *autem*, a great nofe as euer I fawe.
His mafter was wroth, & cride henfe with that dawe.
One faide : talke no more of great nofes ye foole,
Left ye be talkt withall in the whippyng fchoolle.
The foole warnd of great nofes no more to fpeake,
To mend that faut, this way thefe woords did breake.
   Saide I, this is a foule great fpittell nofe ?
Byr lady I lyed, it is a fayre littell nofe.
Will not that foole be had hence (quoth the mafter ?)
Thou wilt foole (quoth one) by walkt with a wafter,
If thou fpeake of any nofe great or fmall.
The foole at thyrd warnyng, mindyng to mend all,
Stept to the boord againe criyng as he gofe,
Before god and man, that man hath no nofe.
The foole was feakt for this : but what of that ?
The great faute here to note, he amended nat:
Whiche is this : not the wife, but the foole ye fée,
In clokyng of one faute, makth fautes two or thrée.

A foole taken for wife. 87.

   Wifdome and foly in thée (as men fcan)
Is as it were a thyng by it felfe foole:
Among fooles thou art taken a wife man,
And among wyfe men, thou art knowne a foole.

Thinges to forbeare. 88.

   Difpleafures that fume and fret
Good to forgeue and forget.
All othes, what whan, and where,
Better forbeare, than forfweare.

P iij

Other

Other mens liuyngis all,
As good forſteale as forſtall,
Not at bottom but at brynke,
Better foreſée, than forthinke.

Of medlars. 89.

To féede of any frute at any feaſt,
Of all kindis of medlers, meddell with the leaſt.
Meddle not with great medlers. For no queſtion,
Medlyng with great medlers, makth yll digeſtion.

Of dwelling. 90.

Betwene Ludgate and Newgate thou canſt dwell neuer,
For in Ludgate or Newgate thou muſt dwell euer.

Of the Milner and the Sexten. 91.

The milner tolth corne, the ſexten tolth the bell,
In whiche tollyng, tollers thriue not a lyke well.
Thon tolth with the clapper, thother in the hopper.
Thone ſauerth of ſyluer, thother ſoundeth of copper.

Of bookes and cheeſe. 92.

No two thinges in all thinges can ſéeme onely one:
Becauſe two thingis ſo, muſt be one thing alone.
How be it readyng of bookes and eatyng of chéeſe,
No two thingis for ſome thingis, more like one then théeſe.
The talent of one cheeſe in mouthes of ten men,
Hath ten different taſts in iudgement moſt times when.
He ſaith tis to ſalt, he ſaith tis to freſhe,
He ſaith, tis to hard, he ſaith tis to neſhe.
It is to ſtrong of the rennet, ſaith hée.
It is ſaith he, not ſtrong enough for mée.
It is ſaith an other, well as can bée.
No two of any ten in one can agrée.
And as they iudge of chéeſe, ſo iudge they of bookes.
On lookers on whiche, who that narowly lookes.
Maie looke for this : Seith he, that booke is to long.
Tis to ſhort ſaith he, Nay, ſaith he, ye ſay wrong,

Tis

Tis of méete length, and for fine phrafe or faire ftile:
The like that booke was not made a good whyle:
And in touchyng the truth inuincibly wrought.
Tis all lies, faith a nother, the booke is nought.
No booke, no chéefe, be it good, be it bad.
But prayfe and difpraife it hath, and hath had.

Of heades. 93.

Some heades haue taken two headis better then one:
But ten heads without wit, I wene as good none.

The woodcocke and the daw. 94.

A woodcocke and a dawe fet vpon a playne,
Both fhewde comparifon eche other to difdaine.
Back (quoth the woodcocke): Straw for the (quoth the dawe)
Shall woodcocks kepe dawes now in dredfull awe?
None awe (quoth the woodcocke) but in behauour
Ye ought to reuerence woodcocks, by your fauour.
For what caufe (quoth the daw?) For your long bils?
Nay (quoth the woodcocke) but lords will by their wils
Rather haue one woodcock, than a thoufand dawfe.
Woodcocks are meate, daws ar carren, wey this claufe.
In déede fir (faide the daw) I muft néedes agrée,
Lords loue to eate you, and not to eate mée.
Caufe of dawes curtefis, fo, if woodcocks thus gather.
Ye fhall haue curtfy: For this I would rather.
Be a daw, and to woodkock curtefy make:
Than be a woodcocke, and of dawes curtefy take.
I were double a daw, had I not leuer,
Byrders fhould (in their byrdyng endeuer)
Take vp gins, and let me go, whan they geat mée,
Than fet gins to get me, for lordes to eate mée.

Of few woordes. 95.

Few woords fhew men wife, wife men doe deuife,
Whiche is oft tyme true, and oft otherwife.

In

In ſome caſe ſilence may as ſtifly ſtand
With folly, as with wiſdome, wiſely ſcand:

Wottyng and weenyng.   96.

Wottyng and wéenyng, were thoſe two thingis one,
Who could wot him ſelfe wiſe like thée, I wene none.

Otherwiſe.

I would geue the beſt fardell in my packe,
To be as wiſe as thou weneſt thou art Iacke.
And to be as wiſe as I wot thou art,
What would I geue troweſt thou ? what ? not a fart.

A much like matter.   97.

Tom, thou thinkſt thy ſelfe wiſe, ye what of that Hew ?
Thou thinkſt thy ſelfe wyſer then I. Ye tom, trew.
It féemth (ſaid a third man) by this deuiſe,
No maiſtry for fooles, to wéene them ſelues wiſe.

Wiſedomė and foly.   98.

Thy wiſedome and foly both, nay no one
Can be conteined in volumes great nor ſmall.
Thy wiſedome beyng none, occupieth place none,
Thy folly beyng all, occupieth place all.

Of lacke.   99.

One lacke of late in thée ſaw wée,
Whiche lackth not now, for this we ſée,
Thou haſt lackt lacke of honeſtée:
But now that lacke lackth not in thée.

                                                            The

The weathercocke, the reede,
and the wynde. 100.

The wethercocke and the réede comparyng late,
Their feruice done to the wynde, fel at debate.
The wynde (quoth the weathercock) windth no where,
But ftreight bolt vpryght I ftand waityng there.
Forfooth faid the réede & where the wynd is found,
At euery blaft I bow downe to the ground.
Surely faid the wynde, the waytyng of the tone,
And curtefie of the tother I take both one.
And none of both good but rather yll to me:
For whan I oft in corners fecrete would be,
Other the crooked curtfy of the réede,
Or weathercockes waytyng, bewraith me with fpéede.
As liefe is to me, in fuch feruyng pretence
Single negligence, as double diligence.
The weathercocke and the réede, beynge both blanke,
Ech told him felfe, much feruice haue fmall thanke.

F I N I S.   Q

Three hundred Epigrammes, vpon three hundred prouerbes,

Inuented and made by
John Heywood.

LONDINI.
1562.

ꝃ The Table of this booke.

Of

The table.

Q iij   Mefure

125

Of

FINIS.

¶Epigrammes vpon prouerbes.

Of amendment.   1.

IF euery man mende one, all fhall be mended.
This meane to amendment, is now intended.
For though no man looke to mend him felf brother:
Yet eche man lookth to controll and mend other.

Wagging of beardes.   2.

It is mery in hall when beardes wagge all.
Hufband for this, thefe woordes to minde I call:
This is ment by men, in their mery eatyng:
Not to wag their beardes in brawlyng and threatyng.
Wyfe, the meanyng herof, differth not twoo pins,
Betwéene waggyng of mens beardes and womens chins.

Of hafte.   3.

The haftie man wanteth neuer woo.
In haftie women not euer foo.
With fuffring hufbandis hafty wiues,
Haue oft we fée, full mery liues.

Breakyng of fquare.   4.

An inche breakth no fquare : which fins thou haft hard tell,
Thou doeft affay how to breake fquare by an ell.

Otherwife.

An inche breakth no fquare : thou breakft none, though it doo.
Thou rather bringft fquare thē breakft fquare betweene too.

Lookyng and leapyng.   5.

Looke er thou leape, nay thou canft in no wife brooke.
To looke er thou leape, for thou leapft ere thou looke.

Weddyng and hanging.   6.

Weddyng and hangyng, are defteny I fée.
Weddyng or hangyng, which is beft, fir (quoth fhée ?)
Forfooth good wife, hangyng I thinke beft (quoth hée)
So helpe me god, good hufband, fo thinketh mée.
Oh how like lambes, man and wyfe here agrée.

R   Of

Of delay. 7.

He that will not when he may,
When he would he ſhall haue nay.
But to that nay, nay I ſay:
If of my wife I delay,
To take ſhroude woordes : yet that ſtay
Stayth them not from me next day.

Of wittes. 8.

So many heades, ſo many wittes, nay nay.
We ſée many heades, and no wittes ſome day.

No lacke in loue. 9.

In loue is no lacke, true I dare be borowe.
In loue is neuer lacke, of ioy or ſorowe.

Otherwyſe.

In loue is no lacke, no in no wooyng day.
But after weddyng day, lets here what ye ſay.

Of homely home. 10.

Home is homely, yea and to homely ſometyme.
Where wiues footeſtooles, to their huſbandes heads clime.

Geuyng and takyng. 11.

Better giue then take, all ſay, but ſo thinke none:
All thinke better take . xx . poundes, then giue one.

Iacke and Gill. 12.

All ſhalbe well, Iacke ſhall haue Gill:
Nay nay, Gill is wedded to wyll.

Of the ende of a wit. 13.

Thou art at thy wits ende, which I wonder in
To ſe a wit at ende before it begin.

Of bought wit. 14.

Wit is neuer good, till it be bought:
Thy wit is dere bought, and yet ſtarke nought.

Otherwyſe.

Wit is neuer good till it be bought Will.
Iacke, to bie or ſell that ware, fooles can no ſkill.

Haſte

130

Of haſte and waſte. 15.

Haſte makth waſte : which perceiued by ſlouth,
Slouth will make no haſte, he ſwerth by his trouth.

Makyng of malte. 16.

Soft fire maketh ſwéete malte, as malt makers tel:
Then to make ſwéete malte, fire is to raſhe in hel.
Wherby ſins in hell no good ale is to ſel,
Drie drunken ſoules can not lyke in hell to dwel.

Of an akyng eye. 17.

Better eye out, then alway ake:
In rage of ache, true as I ſpake:
But in meane ache, meanely to mone,
Better an akyng eye then none.

What thing beggers chooſe. 18.

Beggers ſhould be no choofers, but yet they will:
Who can bryng a begger from choyſe to begge ſtill ?

Of robbyng. 19.

Rob Peter and pay Poule, thou ſayſt I do:
But thou robſt and poulſt Peter and Poule to.

Of neede and law. 20.

Néede hath no law : in ſome caſe in very déede.
Neede hath no law : and yet of law we haue neede.

Of beginnyng and endyng. 21.

Of a harde beginning, comth a good endyng:
Truth, on this terme is not alway dependyng.
Some hardely begin, by the féete to ſit faſt:
That ende with harde hangyng, by the neckes at laſt.

Of grace. 22.

In ſpace comth grace, I graunt grace may come in ſpace:
But in rule, by thy rule neuer looke for grace.

Of fore prouiſion. 23.

Who ſo that knew what would be dere,
Should néede be marchaunt but one yere.

R ij   But

But thou haſt knowen yeres, twoo or thrée:
That good condicions woulde in thée
Both dere and deintely be growen:
And yet for all this, thus fore knowen,
To warne thée of good fore prouiſion,
Thou haſt not now one good condicion.

Of ſaiyng and doyng. 24.

Saying and doyng, are twoo thinges, we ſay:
But thy ſayinges and doynges euery way,
Ioyne iumpe in one thy woordes and déedes procéede:
But thou art good, nother in woorde nor déede.

Of treadyng on a worme. 25.

Treade a worme on the tayle, and it turneth agayne:
But thou tredſt on the wormes head, that to reſtrayne.

Of eaſe in an Inne. 26.

Thou takeſt thine eaſe in thine Inne, ſo nie thée:
That no man in his Inne, can take eaſe by thée.

Otherwyſe.

Thou takeſt thine eaſe in thine Inne, but I ſée:
Thine Inne takth nóther eaſe, nor profit by thée.

How to proue a freende. 27.

Proue thy fréende er thou néede, that canſt thou no way:
For without néede of thy fréende thou art no day.

Vnwiſe weddyng. 28.

Who wedth ere he be wiſe, ſhall die ere he thriue.
Then ſhalt not thou be wedded and riche aliue.

Some thyng and nothyng. 29.

Some thyng is better then nothyng.
In ſome thyng I graunt this othyng:
In ſome I deny : for I ſée
As good haue nothyng, as haue thée.

The ſleapyng dogge. 30.

It is ill wakyng of a ſleapyng dogge.
So thinke many, namely the wrotyng hogge.

It

Of hap. 31.

It hapth in an houre that hapth not in. vii. yéere.
That hapth this houre wife, for thou makſt me good chéere.

Of ſyght and mynde. 32.

Out of ſight out of minde, this may run right:
For all be not in mynde, that be in ſight.

Of mirth with wiſdome. 33.

Tis good to be mery and wyſe:
How ſhall fooles folow that aduyſe?

Of holding of a noſe. 34.

Thou canſt hold my noſe to the gryndſtone:
So can not I thine, for thou haſt none.

An eye ſore. 35.

It is but an eie fore, but an eye ſore, fye
That eye ſore is as yll as any ſore eye.

Of recknyng. 36.

Recknyng without thine hoſte thou muſt recken twyſe:
Maie not my hoſtes diſapoint that deuiſe?

Settyng vp a candell. 37.

To ſet vp a candell before the deuyll.
Dym ſyghted deuyls, I déeme, déeme it not euyll.

Of cloudes and weather. 38.

After clouds blacke, we ſhall haue wether cléere:
And after wether cléere, we ſhall haue cloudes blake:
Now whot, now colde, now fayre, now foule appéere:
As wether cléerth, or cloudth, ſo muſt men take.

Of making and marryng. 39.

Make or mar I wyll, ſo ſaiſt thou euer:
But thou dooſt euer marre, thou makſt neuer.

Of byrdes and byrders. 40.

Better one byrde in hande, then ten in the wood.
Better for byrders, but for byrdes not ſo good.

R iij   Make

Of forowes. 41.

Make not two forowes of one, if thou can:
Left makyng of two forowes, marre one man.

Of feedyng and teaching. 42.

Thou art better fed then taught, I vnder take:
And yet art thou fkyn and bone, leane as a rake.

Of fuffrance. 43.

Of fuffrance comth eafe : how fhall I know that, wyfe ?
I haue fuffred the, without eafe, all my lyfe.

Of him that fet his hand on his money. 44.

Thy hand is on thy halfepeny, and muft Iohn :
For thou haft no more coine to fet thy hand on.

Of a horfe coriyng. 45.

A fhorte hors is foone coride, thatis to wéete,
When fhort hors, and fhort coriers doo méete.

Of fhame. 46.

Shame take him that fhame thinkth, for thou doft thinke non.
Thou art to far paft fhame, fhame to thinke on.

A lordes hart and a beggers purfe. 47.

There is nothing in this world that agréeth wurfe,
Then doth a lordes harte and a beggers purfe,
And yet as yll as thofe two do agrée,
Thou canft not bryng them a funder to bée.

Of fergettyng. 48.

The paryfhe prieft forgeth, he was paryfhe clarke :
And the perfon forgeth, he was parifhe pryfte.
But prieft, clarke, and no clarke, all, who wyll marke,
To forget what we were, fhall fée vs entyfte.

Of the harte and the heele. 49.

Shall I fet at my hart, that thou fettft at thy héele ?
Nay, a hart in a héelde hofe, can neuer do wéele.

Otherwyfe.

Shall I fet at my harte that thou fetft at thy héele ?
Nay, how euer kybde héeles doo, kybd hartis do not wéele.

A man

Praiſe of a man aboue a horſe. 50.

A man may well leade a horſe to the water:
But he can not make him drinke without he lift.
I praiſe the aboue the horſe, in this mater:
For I leadyng the to drynke, thou haſt not miſt
Alway to be ready without reſiſtens
Both to drinke, and be drunke, ere thou were led thens.

Of weeping. 51.

Better children wéepe then olde men, ſay wyſe men.
But olde men wéepe when children laugh, now and then.

Of two falſe knaues. 52.

Two falſe knaues néede no broker : but it is néede
That brokers breake falſe knaues felowſhyp with ſpéede.

A hart in a hoſe. 53.

Thy hart is in thy hoſe, which iayle is not ſtronge,
Thy hoſe are to full of holes, to kepe it longe.

Of creeping and goyng. 54.

Children muſt learne to créepe ere they can go.
In the ſpyttell, olde knaues learne to do ſo.

Of flotyng and fleetyng. 55.

Thou art a flote thou wéenſt, beyng in the fléete:
But flotyng and fléetyng agree not there méete.

A man at an ebbe. 56.

Thou art at an ebbe in Newgate, thou haſt wrong.
But thou ſhalt be a flote at Tyburne ere long.

Syght in a mylſtone. 57.

Thou féeſt far in a mylſtone : thanke God therfore.
Thou féeſt in a milſtone in nothing more.

Of throwyng. 58.

Throw no gyft againe at the gyuers hed :
Namely no gyfte of thy wyfe, geuen in checke.
If thou do, the rebounde may be ſo red,
That the red bloud, may run downe in thy necke.

Store

135

Of ſtore. 59.

Store is no ſore, yes, ſtore may be a ſore.
I thinke it a ſore, of ſores to haue ſtore.

Of one in priſon. 60.

Thou art in by the wéeke, nay ſyr I am here,
Not in by the wéeke, I am in by the yere.

Saintes and deuilles. 61.

Yong ſainte, olde diuell : thers mo of woman kynde:
Then yong deuilles olde ſaintes, in mankynde as I fynde.

Of botching. 62.

God is no botcher, but when God wrought you twoo.
God wrought as like a botcher, as God might doo.

Of a yeres fayre. 63.

The fayre laſtth all the yere, but wyfe I tell thée,
In this yeres fayre, for fayre I can not ſell thée.
I haue woorſe lucke (quoth ſhe) and began to ſcoule,
I can not ſell thée there, for faire nor for foule.

Of a cap and a head. 64.

Thy cappe is better at eaſe then thy hed,
Betwene whiche twayne, might I at wiſhe be ſped,
To chooſe one of the twayne, whiche I would fyrſt craue,
Thy whole cap before thy ſicke hed I woulde haue.

Otherwyſe.

My cap is better at eaſe then my hed.
Thy cap is better then thy hed, tis ſed.

A theefe that hath no felow. 65.

Aſke my felow whether I be a théefe,
No way, can that way, of thy theft make préefe:
Thou haſt no felow in theft : to catche thée:
For there is no théefe (in thefte) can match thée.

Falſe meaſures. 66.

Thou fearſt falſe meaſures, which are thingis to feare ſore:
But I feare falſe meaſures, as much and more.

New

Of cleane sweepyng. 67.

Newe broome swepeth cleane, which is thus vnderstande:
New broome swepeth cleane, in the cleane swepers hande.

Turnyng of typpettes. 68.

He hath turnd his tippet, that turne showth playne,
Our typpets haue ben turnd and turnd agayne.

Otherwyse.

He hath turnd his typpet dyed it and drest it,
Vpon the right syde and feyre and playne prest it.

Otherwise.

He hath turnd his typpet and prest it so close,
That for a turnd typpet it hath a fayre glose.

Otherwise.

He hath turnd his typpet, lord how he prouydes,
Typpetts turnd dyed, shorne, and worne bare on both sydes.

Otherwise.

He hath turnd his typpet, twyse in my syght:
Fyrst on the wronge syde and last on the right.

Otherwyse.

He hath turned his typpet an honest turnyng,
To turne his typpet and turne round for burnyng.

Otherwyse.

He hath turned his typpet shorne agaynst the wull ful,
And more against his will then against the wul.

Otherwyse.

He hath turnd his typpet, that haue we turnd all.
Sum halfe turne, sum hole turne, turnd round as a ball.

Otherwyse.

He hath turnd his typpet, ye for a while:
But might he turne agayne, lord how he wold smyle.

Otherwyse.

He hath turned his typpet, yet mo turns ye mocke,
But who doth weare his typpet a weathercock?

S   He

Otherwyfe. ·
He hath turnd his typpet, now for a noueltée,
And for a noueltée wolde turne ftreyght ageyne he.

Otherwyfe.
He turnth his typpet, or his typpet turnth him,
But which turnth which, I fée not by fwéete faint Sym.

Otherwyfe.
He hath turnd his typpet,
For fymony a fyppet.

Otherwyfe.
He turnth his typpet, if that turnyng turne hym
Into the pulpyt, that turnyng is turnd trym.

Of theft and receite. 69.
Where are no receiuers, there are no théeues:
Where nought is to receiue, theues bryng no gréeues.

Of woorke and play. 70.
As good to play for nought, as to woorke for nought :
But thou wylt play for nought, and not woorke for ought.

Of a peinted fheathe. 71.
Thou makft much of thy peynted fheathe, and wylt do,
It hauynge not one good knyfe longyng therto.

The hare and the hound. 72.
Holde with the hare and run with the hounde, run thare
As wight as the hounde, and as wyfe as the hare.

Of beggers fyngyng. 73.
Beggers fyng before théeues, but what of that ?
When beggers fynge fo, theues fée nought to laugh at.

Of two faces. 74.
Thou bereft two faces in one whood :
Thou haft one yll face, both be not good.

Of beggyng. 75.
Thou begft at wrong doore, and fo haft begd longe :
Thy gettyng by beggyng, fhowth euery doore wrong.

Nothynge

Of nothing. 76.

Nothyng hath no fauer, which fauerles fhowe:
Shewth nothing better, then fum thyng that we knowe.

Otherwyfe.

Nothing hath no fauer, as yl is this othing:
Ill fauerd fumthing, as vnfauerd nothyng.

Of ventring. 77.

Nought venter nought haue, and ventryng of much,
May haue a lyttle, ventryng is now fuch.

Of fhalbe and fhall not be. 78.

That fhalbe, fhalbe. but all that fhulde bée:
Shall not be, nor hath bene, as far as I fée.

The blacke oxe. 79.

The blacke Oxe neuer trode on thy foote:
But the dun Affe hath trode on both thy féete.
Which Affe and thou, may féeme fproong of one roote:
For the affes pace, and thy pace are méete.

Of brydlyng. 80.

I wyll brydell the with rough byt wife. Quoth fhe,
If thou wylt brydell me, I wyll fnafell the.

Mendyng and payryng. 81.

I will mende this houfe, and peyre another.
Ye, but when wylt thou mend thy felfe brother?

Of runnyng without turnyng. 82.

He runth far, that neuer turnth againe : nay nay,
Though the fnayle neuer turne, he runth no far way.

Biyng a pyg. 83.

I will neuer bye the pyg in the poke:
Thers many a foule pyg in a feyre cloke.

Hungry flies. 84.

Hungry flies byte fore, which fhall byte vs euer.
For without hungry flies, we fhalbe neuer.

S ij

Loue

Of louyng a dog. 85.

Loue me, loue my dog : by loue to agrée,
I loue thy dog, as well as I loue thée.

Of precious ſtones. 86.

Folly to caſt precious ſtones before hogs Hewe,
Hodge, except they be precious hogs thou ſayſt trewe.

Otherwyſe.

Caſt precious ſtones before hogs, caſt ſtones to hogs nay,
But precious ſtones haue ben geuen to hogs ſome ſay.

Of yll and good wynde. 87.

It is an yll wynde, that blowth no man to good :
And lyke good wynde, that blowth no man yll.
But fearynge yll wyndes, olde men moſt tymes ſtood.
Out of all extreme wyndes vnder the hyll.

Of ſooth boorde. 88.

Sooth boorde, is no boorde : ſooth boorde ſoundeth yll,
In falſe fayre flattryng boorde : boorde as ye wyll.

Of tales tolde in the eare. 89.

In at the tone eare and out at the tother.
If tales tolde the, go in and out ſo brother,
Then the trauell of thoſe tales ſhewe much woonder :
Thy two eares be two hundred myle a ſunder.

Of goyng. 90.

The further we go, the further behynde.
Méete footemen to go with crabbes, in my mynde.

Otherwyſe.

The further I go, the further behynde.
Stande ſtill foole, tyll thou better footyng fynde.

Of neede. 91.

Néede makth tholde wyfe trot : is ſhe a trotter now ?
Gallop yonge wyues, ſhall tholde trot, out trot you ?

Takyng hart of graſſe. 92.

Thou takeſt hart of graſſe wyfe, not hart of grace.
Cum graſſe, cum grace, ſyr, we graſe both in one place.

Where

Of nothyng and althing. 93.
Where nothing is, a little thyng doth eafe.
Where al thyng is, nothyng can fully pleafe.

Couetyng and leefing. 94.
All couet, all loofe : this comth oft in vre.
But nought haue, nought loofe : this is euer fure.

Of the marche hare. 95.
As mad as a marche hare : where madnes compares:
Are not midfomer hares, as mad as march hares?

How god will not do for vs. 96.
Euery man for him felf, and god for vs all:
God will not feale that writing, write it who fhall?

Of harping on a ftring. 97.
Harpe no more on that ftrynge, for it ftandth to hie:
And foundeth as bafely as a halter, wel nie.

A loffe by the deuils death. 98.
The deuill is dead, then haft thou loft a fréende.
In all thy doinges, the deuill was at tone ende.

Otherwife.
The deuill is dead, one deuill is dead but wée fe:
Mo deuils left aliue, as ill or worfe then he.

Otherwife.
The deuill is dead, who fhall enherite his lande:
Inowe, the deuill hath left children a thoufande.

Otherwyfe.
The deuill is dead, who fhall his land rightly win,
Thou, for thou by condifhin, art next of kin.

Otherwife.
The deuill is dede, nay the deuill is in a fowne,
But the deuill reuiueth agayne, chil ley my gowne.

Otherwife.
The deuill is dead, what helpeth the death of the deuill,
The deuill hath heyres as ill as he, and more euill.

S iij   He

Of a fheepes iye. 99.

He caſt a fhéepes eye at her : a ſtraunge eye fpred,
To fe a fhéepes eye, looke out of a calues hed.

Of rule. 100.

Better rule, then be rulde : wife thy endeuer,
Hath fhewde thée to be rulde, by that rule euer.

Of blinde bayard. 101.

Who fo bolde as blinde bayerd : no beaſt of trouth.
Wherof my bolde blinde bayerd, perfit proofe fhouth,
Both of his boldnes, and for his bolde blindnes.
By late occaſion, in a caufe of kindnes :
A company of vs, rode in certaine grounde :
Where we welny, an impaſſible flough founde.
Their horfes, ere they entred began to ſtay.
Euery one horfe geuyng an other the way.
Of good manner as it were, and more and more,
Eche horfe gaue backe, to fet his better before.
Saue this rude ruſtie, bolde blinde bayerd of mine,
As rafhely, as rudely, chopt foorth : and in fine,
Without any curtſie , ere any man bids :
Blindly and boldly, he lepte into the mids.
And looke how boldly, the mids he lept in till,
Euen with like boldnes, in the mids he lay ſtill :
And trow you the Iade, at the beſt mens wordes theare,
Woulde ſtur one ioynte : nay not the breade of one heare.
But ſtarde on them, with as bolde a countenaunce :
As that hole had ben his, by enheritaunce :
He hauyng no more to do there then had I.
But ſtreight there cumth, a carteweare, of good hors by :
By force wherof, and helpe of all that rout,
Blinde bayerd and I, were drawen together out.
Which blinde boldenes, by this admonicion :
Except he amend in fome méete condicion,

Rather

Rather then ride fo, I will a foote take payne,
Blynde bolde bayerd, fhall not thus beare me againe.
Of the fpinfters thrift.   102.
Thus rideth the rocke . if the rocke be ridyng,
The fpinfters thrift, is fet a foote flidyng.
Of defenes.   103.
Who is fo deafe, as he that will not heare:
Not the deuill, till will draw his hearyng neare.
Of a good hors.   104.
It is a good hors, that neuer ftumbleth.
Then haue I a good hors, for my hors tumbleth.
And fauleth downe right, my hors ftumbleth neuer.
So well am I horft, and haue bin horft euer.
And fo loth to lend him, to féelde or townes éende.
That as foone fhall my fo ride him, as my fréende.
Of waies to the wood.   105.
There be mo wayes to the wood then one.
Of all good wayes to wood, thou gofte none.
Of one that may foone amend.   106.
He may foone amend, for he can not apeyre.
A good euidence to proue him the deuils heyre.
An ill hearer.   107.
I can not heare on that fide, no, trueth to tell:
Of any fide, thou couldft neuer yet heare well.
Of a good face.   108.
I did fet a good face on the matter Ione,
Thou didft borow it then Bes, for thou haft none.
A fharpe thorne.   109.
It prickth betimes, that fhalbe a fharpe thorne.
I wéene thou prickft wife, ere time thou were borne.
Commyng and goyng.   110.
As faft as one goth, an other cumth in vre.
Twoo buckets in a well, come and go fo fure.

                                        But

But go or cum, who ſhall, while all come and go:
Seldome cumth the better, practiſe préeueth ſo.

The better cumth ſeldome. 111.

Séeldome cumth the better, come or go who will,
One nayle driueth out an other, wée ſe ſtill.

One driueth out an other. 112.

One nayle driueth out an other, with ſtrokes ſo ſtout:
That the hammer hed which driueth them, werth quite out.

Of burden. 113.

Light burden , far heuy : that dooſt thou try.
A fether borne far, will tyre thée welnie.

Otherwiſe.

Light burden far heuy, borne for other men:
For our ſelues, heuy burdens light inough then.

Otherwiſe.

Light burden, far heuy, thy braine lacketh ſtrength
To beare a pinte of wine, a payre of buttes length.

Otherwiſe.

Light burden, far heuy, thou dooſt finde that lacke:
In all light good burdens, that lie on thy backe.

Otherwiſe.

Light burden, far heuy, how can lame folke proue,
Who in all their liues, their lengthes do not remoue.

Runnyng and goyng. 114.

He may ill run, that can not go:
He that ſitth by the féete, finde ſo.

A lacke of tooles. 115.

What is a workeman without his tooles.
How may bables be miſt among fooles.

Taſt of a mans tales. 116.

A tale of a tub, thy tales taſte all of ale.
Not of peſcod ale, ſyr, my tales are not ſtale.

A cat

Of a cattes looke. 117.

A cat may looke on a kyng, and what of that.
When a cat fo lookth : a cat is but a cat.

One put out of a creede. 118.

Thou maift be in my pater nofter in déede.
But furely thou fhalt neuer come in my créede.
I care not, though I do not, what can I win,
To come in a créede, whiche créede god is not in.

All that may be won of the fox. 119.

Wée can haue no more of the Fox but the fkin:
And the Foxe thinketh that, to much for vs to win.

The fuertie of fome fcale. 120.

As fure as it were fealde with butter, for footh:
Sum butter feale laftth, as longe as fome waxe dooth.

The hares goyng away. 121.

There goth the Hare away, is fhe gone fay you?
Let her go, we haue Hares, and hare heds ynou.

Iudgement of colours. 122.

Blinde men fhould iudge no coloures : fhould they nat?
Blinde men will iudge all colours, for all that.

Hap and wit. 123.

Better be happy then wife, here art thou hit,
Thy hap hath euer ben better, then thy wit.

Otherwyfe.

Better be happy then wyfe, not fo, fum fay:
He that can be wife, fhalbe happy, fay thay.

Of fortune to fooles. 124.

God fendth fortune to fooles, not to euery chone:
Thou art a foole, and yet fortune thou haft none.

Otherwyfe.

God fendth fortune to fooles, and to wife men ftill.
God fendth good fortune, or the deuill fendth ill.

T   Let

Of loofers wordes. 125.

Let the loofers haue their wordes, all at onfe:
Shall the loofers talke? there will be chat for the nonfe.

Gettyng and spendyng. 126.

Ill gotten ill fpent: be that tale true to tell,
Thou art neuer lyke to fpende peny well.

Matters not leyde a water. 127.

My matter is leyde a water, thats a falfe tale:
Thy matters lie not in water, they lie in ale.

Meafure. 128.

Meafure is a mery meane.
Which filde with noppy drinke.
When mery drinkers drinke of cleane:
Then merely they winke.

Otherwife.

Meafure is a mery meane,
But I meane meafures gret:
Where lippes to litell pitchers leane:
Thofe lippes they fcantly wet.

Otherwife.

Meafure is a mery meane.
But ynche, foote, yerde, or ell:
Thofe meafures are not worth a beane:
They meafure no drinke well.

Otherwife.

Meafure is a mery meane.
Be drinke deare or good cheape:
From meafure no wight, may thée weane:
Thou meafurft drinke by heape.

Otherwife.

Meafure is a mery meane.
Good licker may not fhrinke:
Thou takft no triacle of Geane
So holfome as good drinke.

Meafure

Otherwyfe.
Meafure is a mery meane.
Shewyng indifferency:
Would thale wife, play the poulyng queane:
Yet meafure will not lie.
Otherwife.
Meafure is a mery meane.
That doth diligently:
Attend the tappes of ftande and fteane:
To moyft thy lippes full dry.
Otherwyfe.
Meafure is a mery meane.
And meafure is thy mate,
To be a deacon, or a deane:
Thou wouldft not chaunge the ftate.
Otherwife.
Meafure is a mery meane.
Who that fhall enterprife,
This meafure from thée, for to gleane,
Right erly muft he rife.
Otherwife.
Meafure is mery meane.
In volewmes full or flat,
There is no chapter, nor no feane,
That thou applieft like that.

Goyng beyonde the wall. 129.
Furder then the wall, we can not go,
Thine vfage fhowth otherwife, then fo:
Thou gofte, when thou muft ftart out of fight:
To the wall, and ouer the wall quight.

Of harme. 130.
A man far from his good, is nie his harme,
Ny thy good, next thy harme, as chaunce may charme.

T ij   A man

Otherwyfe.

A man far from his good, is nie his harme,
For thée to feare that, it were worfe then woodnes.
Mouables, vnmouables, lande or farme,
Thou haft not one grotes woorth, of good or goodnes.

Otherwyfe.

A man far from his good, is nie his harme.
This fhewth the nie harme : for hadft thou an arme
That could and wolde, reache hence to Conftantine,
That arme coulde not reache to any good of thine.

Wit kept by warmth. 131.

Thou art wyfe inough, if thou kéepe thée warme:
But the leaft colde that cumth, kilth thy wit by harme.

Light comyng and goyng. 132.

Light cum, light go, that cumth in vre by light féete:
But light heds, make light féete, ly lame in the ftréete.

Otherwyfe.

Light cum, light go, for that thou art well wrought:
For thou art as light, as a thyng of nought.

Otherwyfe.

Light cum, light go, pas, cum and go lightly,
In a Iuggler, that lightnes is fightly.

Otherwyfe.

Light cum, light go, thy light goyng doth excell:
But thy light comyng, I like not half fo well.

Of kiffing. 133.

Unknowen vnkift, and beyng knowen I wéene,
Thou art neuer kift, where thou mayft be feene.

Otherwyfe.

Vnknowen vnkift, from that defyre, wife blys thée,
For no man that féeth thée, defireth to kis thée.
From kyffyng in fight hufbande, fuch as flée mée,
Let them come kis me, where they do not fe mée.

Leaue

Of leaue. 134.

Leaue is light, lyght inough as thou wilt make it,
If thy maiſter geue no leaue thou wilt take it.

Otherwyſe.

Leaue is light, ye and leaue is axed lyghtly,
And may be graunted lightly, axyd rightly.

God in the almery. 135.

There is god in thalmery, a well playde part.
Shut god in thine almery, out of thy hart.

The diuell in thorologe. 136.

The diuell is in thorologe, the houres to trye,
Searche houres by the ſunne, the deuyls dyall wyll lye.

Otherwyſe.

The deuyll is in thorologe, nowe chéere in boules:
Let the deuyl kepe our clockes, whyle god kéepe our ſoules.

The beſt. 137.

The beſt is behynde, the woorſt is before:
Betwene bothe, beware dryft to the woorſt ſhore.

Otherwiſe.

The best is behynde, we go before to faſt,
Byde for the beſt, els it will be loſt at laſt.

Otherwiſe.

The beſt is behynde, ſtarte thou backe and fet it,
Abyde abyde, a wyſer man muſt get it.

Otherwyſe.

The beſt is behinde, euen ſo I thought it wolde:
The beſt lacketh féete, foote pace with vs to holde.

Otherwyſe.

The beſt is behynde, behynde nor yet before:
Wolde I haue the beſt, but with vs euermore.

The woorſt. 138.

The woorſt is behynde.
There art thou aſſynde.

T iij   The

149

Otherwyſe.

The woorſt is behinde, but the way is not rough:
The woorſt wyll get before agayne, tyme ynough.

Otherwyſe.

The woorſt is behynde, yet behynde woorſe euyll?
We ſée our fare, at next courſe, cumth the deuyll.

Otherwiſe.

The woorſt is behynde, god kepe it behinde vs.
Or vs before it, as it neuer fynde vs.

Laſtyng of woonder.   139.

A woonder laſteth but. ix. daies:
Yes thou dydſt. ix. yeres gon
But one good déede, for whiche ſum ſaies,
Thou art yet woondred on.

Of a galde horſe.   140.

Rub a galde horſe on the backe and he wyll kycke:
But the galde aſſe wyll ſtande ſtyll, rub, ſpur, or pricke.

Good begynnyng and ende.   141.

Of a good begynnyng, there cumth a good éende:
Nay, Lucyfer began well, and now a féende.
But of good begynnyng and endyng, truth to tell,
The beſt way to ende well, is to begyn well.

The ſtill ſoowe.   142.

The ſtyll ſowe eath all the draffe, my ſowe eath none,
The deuill ſtylth not my ſowe, tyll hir groyne be gone.

Of ſtumblyng.   143.

Stumble at a ſtrawe, and leape ouer a blocke,
Such ſtumblers are blockeheads, or els they do mocke:

Otherwiſe.

Stumble at a ſtrawe, and leape ouer a blocke,
The Aſſe and the Ape, ſeme here ioyned in one ſtocke.

Of the ſhoe and the ſole.   144.

The ſhooe wyll holde with the ſole. No man knowth it,
But he that knowth, how the ſhomaker ſowth it.

The

Otherwyfe.

The fhooe wyll holde with the fole, what fhulde the fhoo doo,
But holde with the fole, the fole will holde with the fhoo.

Myght and ryght. 145.

Myght ouercumth ryght. God kepe vs from that myght,
God geue vs that might, that ftryueth not with ryght.

Byrth and teaching. 146.

Better vnborne then vntaught, but of truth, thow
Were as well taught afore thou were borne, as now.

Of hangyng. 147.

I haue hangd vp my hatchet . and fcapte thy felfe ?
Thou fhuldeft rather be hangde, then thy hatchet, elfe.

An olde knaue. 148.

An olde knaue is no babe, no. but we knowe,
Of an olde knaues babe, an olde knaue may growe.

A mans heare and his whood. 149.

Thy heare growth through thy whood . is thy whood torne ?
Or dooth thy heare perfe through thy whood, lyke a horne.

Geynes and loffes. 150.

Lyght geynes, make heauy purfes.
Lyght loffes make heauy curfes.

Otherwyfe.

Light geynes make heuy purfes, and lyght purfes
Make heauy hartes, and heuy harted curfes.

Otherwyfe.

Light geynes make heuy purfes, fo brag marchantes bare,
When they take thrée halfpence, for two peny worth ware.

Theeues fallyng out. 151.

When théeues fall out, trewe men come to their goode.
Cum betymes, or els it is gone by roode.

Of a fhorne face. 152.

Thy face is fhorne ageynft the wull, very déepe,
Haue I wool in my face ? ye, thou art a fhéepe.

Thou

A benche whiſtler. 153.

Thou art a benchwhiſtler. a ſhryll whyſtlyng wenche,
But how long haſt thou whiſtled in the kynges benche,
I haue whyſtled in the kynges bench (Gefrey)
As longe as thou haſt marcht in the Marſhalſey.

What god ſeyde to one. 154.

Thou art one of them, to whom god bad who,
God tooke the for a carte horſe, when god bad ſo.

Otherwiſe.

Thou art one of them, to whom god bad who,
I wéene thou wentſt to far, when god bad ſo.

Boowyng and breakyng. 155.

Better boowe then breake, when ſtrainyng ſhall ſtretche.
Nay, as good breake as boowe, beynde our retche.

Otherwyſe.

Better boowe then breake, I praiſe this that ye ſpeake,
But ſum bend, or be bent and boude, tyll they breake.

Otherwiſe.

Better boowe then breake, it is truly ſpoken.
Boude wands ſerue for ſumwhat, ſo do not broken.

Of wreſtlyng. 156.

The weaker hath the woorſe, in wreſtlyng alway,
Beſt for the weake to leaue wreſtlyng then I ſay,

God and the church. 157.

The neare to the churche, the furder from god,
Bothe one to thée, a reame thence, or a rod.

Of one tale in all men tolde. 158.

It muſt néedes be true, that euery man ſaith,
Tyll all men ſay one thinge, the iudgement ſtaith.

Otherwiſe.

It muſt nedes be true that euery man ſaith,
Muſt it ſo ? then art thou a foole, in fayth.

Of malkin. 159.

There be mo maydes then Malkyn, thou ſaiſt truth Ione.
But how may we be ſure, that Malkin one ?   I will

Raſhe ventringe. 160.

I will ſet all, euen at ſyxe and at ſeuen,
Ye, and repent all, betwene ten and eleuen.

A ſcabde horſe. 161.

A ſcabde horſe is good enough, for a ſcalde ſquyre.
Your maſterſhyp, nede not care, what horſe ye hyre.

Of ſyttyng. 162.

Betwéene two ſtooles, my tayle goth to the grounde.
Better ſtande then ſyt, tyll ſure ſeate be founde.

Ale and wyt. 163.

When ale is in, wyt is out.
When ale is out, wyt is in.
The fyrſt thou ſhewſt, out of dout,
The laſt in the hath not byn.

Of reſtitucion. 164.

Steale a gooſe, and ſticke downe a fether.
In a fether, and ſuch conſcience,
If I ſhoulde ſtycke them downe together:
I can deuyſe no great difference.

Eatyng of flies. 165.

The blynde eateth many a flie, not thou wife,
For though blyndnes haue banyſht thyne eyes defence,
Yet when flies in flienge to thy mouth be ryfe,
Thy toung is a flie flap, to flap flies from thence.

Of the foxes preaching. 166.

When the foxe preacheth, then beware our géefe.
You that feare your géefe, learne wyt here a péefe.
Kepe foxes from pulpets, your géefe to teache:
Or kepe géefe from ſermons, when foxes do preache.

Of poore mens ſoules. 167.

Poore men haue no ſoules, no but poore men had ſoules:
Tyll the drunken ſoules, drownd theyr ſoules in ale boules.

U   Poore

Otherwyfe.

Poore men haue no foules, yes, but we fée,
Poore men foules as poore : as their purfes bée.

Otherwyfe.

Poore men haue no foules, no. haue ryche men any,
I feare but fewe, for they haue loft foules many.

Otherwife.

Poore men haue no foules. No no. the dyuell mad them.
The fots coulde not kepe theyr foules, whyle they had them.

Promife of lycence. 168.

I wyll fay no more, tyll the day be longer,
No no, fay no more tyll thy wyt be ftronger.

Of little faiyng. 169.

Lyttle fayde, foone amended.
Lyttle good, foone fpended.
Lyttle charge, foone attended.
Lyttle wyt, foone ended.

Of the tyde. 170.

The tyde taryeth no man. but here to fcan,
Thou art tyde fo, that thou taryft euery man.

Praife of good ende. 171.

All is well that endth well, a good faiynge (wyfe)
But I would fée it proued, by thende of thy lyfe.

Of hearyng and iudgeyng. 172.

Here all parts, ere ye iudge any.
God fende fuche hearers many.

A leffon for lookyng. 173.

Sum man may better Steale a horfe :
Then fum may ftand and looke vpone.
Where fuche fufpicion ftandth in force,
Flée fyght of ftolne horfe, looke on none.

Of a womans liues. 174.

Wyfe, a woman hath nine liues lyke a cat.
Syr, you haue but one lyfe, and yet inough of that.

I wyll

The crowe called white. 175.

I wyll fay the crowe is whyte . art thou fo lyght,
What is thy credence, when the crowe cumth in fyght.

Otherwyfe.

Ye muft fay the crowe is whyte, in any cafe,
Not nowe, but we were made fey fo a longe fpace.

Otherwyfe.

I will fay the crowe is whyte. wylt thou fo?
When euery man féeth hir blacke : go foole go.

Of the olde foole. 176.

There is no foole to the olde foole.
Go yonge fooles, to tholde fooles to fcoole.

Otherwyfe.

There is no foole to tholde foole : fpeake not that loude,
That prayfe wyll make olde fooles vengeable proude,
Which prayfe of olde fooles, yong fooles perceyuyng playne:
Yonge fooles, and olde fooles, eche wyll other difdayne.

Of a beane. 177.

A beane in a monkes whood, very good,
Here is the beane, but where is the whood.

The gyft of a pyg. 178.

Syr ye gyue me a pyg, of myne owne fowe.
Wyfe, I gyue a fowe pyg to a fowe nowe.

Chaunge and robery. 179.

Chaunge is no robry, that is a tale not ftraunge,
Chaunge is no robry, but robry maketh chaunge.
Many fwéete blyffynges chaunge to bytter curfes.
When trewe mens money, chaungth into théeues purfes.

Of fayre woordes. 180.

Fayre woordes make fooles fayne, that was by olde scooles:
But now we fée, fayre woordes make wyfe men fooles.

Otherwyfe.

Fayre woords make fooles fayne, yet fayre woordis are chereful,
But foule woordis make all folke, Irefull or ferefull.

U ij   I laught

Of laughyng. 181.

I laught in my fléeue, feynt laughynges there to wyn,
Sléeues be to narowe, to laugh luſtily in.

Of ſeekyng. 182.

I féeke for a thyng wyfe, that I would not fynde.
Good huſbande ye are the more foole in my mynde.

Otherwiſe.

Thou féekeſt for a thynge, that thou wouldſt not fynde.
And I fynde all thynges, that I do not féeke:
In my hap, and thy wyt, what dyffrence aſſynde,
I wéene not the value of a good gréene léeke.

Of a head vnder a gyrdell. 183.

He hath thy hed vnder his gyrdell, take héede
He hange not thy hed, in his gyrdell in déede.

Of wyde ſhootyng. 184.

He ſhooteth wyde. the cauſe why, I fée euen ſyth.
He hath not one ſtreight ſhafte, to ſhoote ſtreight with.

Otherwiſe.

He ſhootth wyde.
On which ſyde.

Otherwiſe.

He ſhooteth wyde, but he can not amende that,
For he féeth not the marke that he ſhooteth at.

The fooles bolte. 185.

A fooles bolte is foone ſhot, and fléeth oftymes fer,
But the fooles bolte and the marke, cum few tymes ner.

Of a marchant. 186.

He is a marchaunt without money or ware.
Byd that marchaunt be couered, he is bare.

Otherwyſe.

He is a marchaunt without money or ware.
He hath in ſum reſpecte, the leſſe cauſe of care.

Tounge

Of tongue. 187.

Tounge breaketh bone, and bone it hath none.
I wiſhe (wife) thy tounge may haue a bone.
And I wiſhe (quoth ſhe) a bone in your whood.
Wyſhe that bone away (ſaid he) tis not good.
Then wiſhe you the tother (quoth ſhe) away.
They did ſo, which doone : now ſayd ſhe wée may
Witnes bothe, that you haue your wiſhe in fine,
But both can not witnes that I haue mine.

Otherwyſe.

Tounge breaketh bone, it ſelfe hauyng none.
Such tounges ſhould haue bones, or bodkins the tone.

Otherwyſe.

Toung breaketh bone, and bone it ſelf hath none.
Yes, thy tounge is full of good ale bones (Ione)

Of ſpeeche. 188.

Spare to ſpeake, ſpare to ſpéede. If ſpéeche bring ſpéede,
Then wilt thou ſpéede, for thou ſpeakſt more then néede.

A buſy body. 189.

He will haue an ore in euery mans barge.
Euen in cocke lorels barge, he berth that charge.

Otherwyſe.

He will haue an ore in euery mans barge,
Then with ſum of thoſe ores, he rowth at large.

Of time. 190.

Time is tickell, we may matche time in this,
For we be euen as tickell, as time is.

Otherwyſe.

Time is tickell.
Chaunce is fickell.
Man is brickell.
Freilties pickell.
Poudreth mickell,
Seaſonyng lickell.

U iij   He

157

Of far caſtyng. 191.

He caſth beyonde the moone . great diuerſitie,
Betwéene far caſtyng and wiſe caſtyng, may be.

Otherwiſe.

He caſth beyonde the moone . what néede that be doone?
We haue caſtyng inough, a this ſide the moone.

Of hunger. 192.

Hunger droppeth out of his noſe,
That is the woorſt kinde of the poſe.

Of feedyng. 193.

He hath fed till he is as full as a toon.
I meane an emptie toon . what foode hath he woon?

Of Mortimers ſow. 194.

Backare, quoth Mortimer to his ſow.
Went that ſow backe, at that biddyng trowe you?

Otherwiſe.

Backare quoth Mortimer to his ſow : ſe
Mortimers ſow ſpeakth as good latin as he.

Otherwiſe.

Backare quoth Mortimer to his ſowe :
The bore ſhall backe firſt (quoth ſhe) I make a vowe.

Of fleabytyng. 195.

Tis but a fleabityng : fréende if fleas bite ſo,
They will bite men to the bare bones where they go.

The breecheleſſe maiſter. 196.

The maſter weareth no breeche, then I proteſt,
The maſter is a girle, a boy, or a beſt.

Of meate and ſauce. 197.

Swéete meate will haue foure ſauce, to this reaſon feate,
Ioyne this conuerſion foure ſauce will haue ſwéete méate.
Thus ſourenes and ſwéetenes, the one and thother,
In feare of the tone, we hope of the tother.

Swéete

Otherwife.
Swéete meate will haue foure fauce, where that is féene,
As good lacke that meate, as haue that fauce, I wéene.

Of proferd feruice. 198.
Proferde feruice ftinketh, thou art deceiued elfe,
Thy proferde feruice ftinkth not : thou ftinkft thy felfe.

Otherwyfe.
Proferde feruice ftinkth . more foole thou to profer it,
Thou fhuldeft feafon thy feruice ere thou offer it.

Of common medlers. 199.
He that medleth with all thyng, may fhooe the goflyng :
If all fuch medlers were fet to goofe fhoyng :
No goofe néede go barfote betwene this and Gréefe,
For fo : we fhould haue as many goofe fhooers as géefe.

Of enough and a feaft. 200.
As good ynough as a feaft : ye god faue it.
Inough were euen as good, if we might haue it.

Otherwife.
As good ynough as a feaft.
This for a truth fay moft and leaft.
But what ynough is iuftly ment,
And with inough to be content,
Thofe are twoo pointes that fewe or none,
Can learne to know, and ftande vpon.

Of plaine fafhion. 201.
The playne fafhin is beft, what plaine without pleates
That fafhin commendth the calfe when it bleates.

Otherwife.
The playne fafhin is beft, and accepted befte
In thinges that pleafe heares but not in the reft.

Otherwife.
The playne fafhin is beft, thats trewly expreft
Where fafhiners of playne fafhins are honeft.

He

Of him that cumth laſt. 202.
He that cumth laſt make all faſt, to this ſay ſum
All is made faſt ere the laſt cummer cum.

Otherwyſe.
He that cumth laſt make all faſt,
Who ſhall make him faſt that cumth laſt.

Of ſtriuyng. 203.
He ſtriueth agaynſt the ſtreme, by cuſtums ſcoole
That ſtriuer is either a fiſhe or a foole.

Of ſittyng. 204.
Better ſit ſtill then riſe and fall
If all ſayle ye may hange when ye ſhall.

Of writyng to frendes. 205.
Ye may write to your fréendes that ye are in helth:
Who may write to his fréendes that he is in welth.

Of great clarkes. 206.
The greateſt clarkes be not the wiſeſt men
Be ſmaule learnd or vnlernd fooles wyſeſt then.

Of killyng. 207.
He will kill a man for a meſſe of muſtard
He will kill ten men then for a cuſtard.

Of falſhed. 208.
There is falſhed in felowſhip, there is ſo
The felowſhyp is ſmall els as the worlde doth go.

Otherwyſe.
There is falſhed in felowſhip, no wunder
Falſhed and felowſhip are féeld a ſunder.

Of bleedyng. 209.
Here lithe all and bleadth, all, thats fals and fooliſh,
Thou neuer ſawſt bloud bléed out of a ſtockfiſh.

Of ſeyng. 210.
Séeſt me and féeſt me not, both one thing for ſoth
As good vnſéene as ſéene whoſe ſight no good doth.

Of

Of ils. 211.

Of twoo Ils chofe the leaſt, of ils many
The leaſt is to great to chofe any.

Otherwyfe.

Of two Ils chofe the leaſt, may we choofe ils now,
Choofe on choofers the like choyfe neuer had yow.

Of Pepper. 212.

Thou takſt pepper in the nofe, and yet thy nofe,
Lookth not blacke like pepper, but red like the rofe.

Otherwyfe.

Thou takſt pepper in the nofe which néedeth not,
Thy nofe without pepper is firy red whot.

Otherwyfe.

Thou takſt pepper in the nofe which fo fefond
Shewth thy nofe better fefond then thy hed refónd.

Of an ill ſtake. 213.

An ill ſtake that can not ſtand one yere in a hedge
If the ſtake felf fayle, the ſtake is as ye alege.
But if ſtake ſtoobbers will not let ſtakis ſtand
Blame not the ſtake, blame the ſtake ſtoobbers hand,

Of ſuffraunce. 214.

Suffrans is no quittans, but fuffryng to longe,
Showth much like a quittans in fuffryng of wrong.

Of miſrecknyng. 215.

Miſrecknyng is no paiment, yes as doth fall
In fum reckners, miſrecknyng is payment all.

Otherwife.

Miſrecknyng is no payment, to auoyde that,
Sum detters with their creditours recken nat.

Of euen recknyng. 216.

Euen reeknyng makth long fréends
Od recknyng makth many féends.

Of takyng. 217.

I will take as falth in the ſheafe, where euer it fall
In the ſheafe or out of the ſheafe thou takſt all.

X   Mum

Of mum. 218.

Mum is counfell in euery man we fée
But mum except, nothyng is counfell in thée.

Of ftoppyng a mouth. 219.

He fhall not ftop my mouth, no Nan I thinke that
I beleue all the deuils in hel ftopth it nat.

Of caftyng. 220.

He is caft in his owne turne, that is likly
And yet in all turnes he turnth wonders quikly.

Of Iacke. 221.

He is iacke out of office, curtfie withdrawe
Iacke once out of office all hayle Iack dawe.

Of the winking Cat. 222.

Let the Cat winke and let the Moufe run, run mife
Or els the cats clawes will catch you at a trife.

Otherwyfe.

Let the cat winke and let the moufe run, run rats
Smalle holes kéepe fmall mife, from wily winkyng cats.

Otherwyfe. ,

Let the cat winke and let the moufe run, créepe moufe créepe
Run not before cats that winke more then they fléepe.

Of faying nay. 223.

Say nay and take it, ye fay nay and take it
But fay nay or fay ye neuer forfake it.

Otherwyfe.

Say nay and take it, here me fay this othyng
Say nother ye nor nay, takte and fay nothyng.

Of the pie and crowe. 224.

Not to hie for the pie nor to lowe for the crowe
Hie pies made lowe crowes we haue inough I trowe.

Of faying nought but mum. 225.

I will fay nought but mum.
Thou fhowft the more wit fum.

I

Otherwyfe.
I wyll fay nought but mum, that I befeeche,
Mum hath a grace in thee far more then fpeeche.

Of tounge and wit. 226.
Thy tounge runth before thy wit, thats no rafhe rafe
For fo may it run, runnyng but a fnayle pace.

Of owne. 227.
Owne is owne,
Whers owne knowne.

Otherwyfe.
Owne is owne, thefe wordes I fpeke with eyes weepyng,
For all mine owne is in other mens keepyng.
But good is that riches where it is heapt
That from thowner by no means can be keapt.

Of fpinnyng. 228.
She hath fpun a fayre threede, which fhowth in deede
That a fowle fpinner may fpin a fayre threede.

Of laughyng. 229.
They laugh that win, falfly to win and keepe,
Winners may laugh when they haue caufe to weepe.

Otherwyfe.
They laugh that win, by theft to win and keepe
Theeues at ftealyng laugh, theeues at hangyng weepe.

Of pleying. 230.
He pleyth beft that wins, that deny I will
Many pleyers win much that pley very ill.

Otherwyfe.
He pleyth beft that wins, there is a lye runnyng,
Many win much, much more by hap then cunnyng.

Of the winde blowyng. 231.
Let this winde ouerblow, when ouer blow
This winde will ouer blow vs firft I trow.

                    X ij   I haue

Of far and nie. 232.

I haue féene as far come as nie, come no nere
The ferder thou art hence the better is it here.

Of thynftep. 233.

He is hie in thynftep, his fteps may be hie,
But to ftepe in good fteps he ftepth nothyng nie.

Of fmaule and greate. 233.

Many fmaul make a great, and fum great made fmall,
Thou hadft great good maners, and thou haft non at all.

Of the keyfe. 234.

The keife hang not all by one mans gyrdle, no
Euery key hath a clog, who wolde be clogd fo.

Of prouender. 236.

His prouender prickth him, prick him godsforbod
What is his prouender, pinnes by likelyhod.

Otherwyfe.

His prouender prickth him, where grewe that corne,
Pricking prouender as il as botes borne.

Otherwyfe.

His prouender prickth him, that hors muft néede ftur
Prickt, with in with prouender, without with fpur.

Of fum here and there. 237.

Here fum and there fum, ye here and there fum:
But moft when and moft where no fum doth cum.

Of the perfons lemman. 238.

She is as tender as a perfons leman,
Parfons lemans are tough inough now and than.

Of il weede. 239.

Ill wéede growth faft, it groweth faft in déede
The corne can fcantly growe for the wéede.

Otherwyfe.

Ill wéede growth faft, that is fhowyng
In the fhow of thy faft growyng.

He

Of fynkyng. 240.

He fhall fynke in his owne finne. ye when he fynkth,
But he fléeeth in his owne fin yet me thinkth.

Of good fyluer. 241.

She thinkth hir farthing good fyluer, but truft me
She is quycke fyluer what euer hir farthyng be.

Of the proude cocke. 242.

Euery cocke is proude on his owne dunghyll,
The hen is proud inough there marke who wyll.

Of fat in the fyre. 243.

The fat is in the fyre, that is a fhrewde turne,
Caft the leane after, fat and leane let all burne.

Of bowe bent. 244.

I haue the bent of his bowe, that I know.
What bolts fhootft thou from that bow, fooles bolts I trow.

Of gods beynge. 245.

God is where he was. ye but fo art not thow
Thou were abrode late and art in Newgate now.

Of kinffolke. 246.

Many kynffolke fewe fréendis,
Fewe fréendis and many féendis.

Of Freendfhippe. 247.

A fréende is neuer knowne tyll a man haue néede
Nor then nother for any I know in déede:

Of nothinge. 248.

Where nothyng is the kynge muft léefe his ryght,
Where althynge is there ryght is loft by myght.

Of pouertee. 249.

Pouertée partth felowfhip, thats not trewe euer,
Pouertie in beggers partth felowfhip neuer.

Of eares glowyng. 250.

Thyne eares may glowe, lets fée whether they glow Iohn.
I lye : thyne eares can not glowe for thou haft non.

X iij   Toft

Of poſte and pyller. 251.

Toſt from poſt to pyller, thou art a pyller ſtronge,
And thou haſt byn a pyller ſum ſay to longe.

Of may be. 252.

Be as be may is no bannynge.
But be as be ſhall hath much ſcannynge.

Of vſe. 253.

Vſe maketh maſtry, that is a trew tale to tell,
In that vſe hath made the pycke a purſe ſo well.

Of ſpurnyng. 254.

Folly to ſpurne or kycke agenyſt the harde wall.
Beyng ſhod with cakebred, that ſpurner marth all.

Otherwyſe.

Folly to ſpurne or kycke ageynſt the harde wall,
But ageynſt ſoft walles ſpurners ſpurne and kyck all.

Of tiyng the bell. 255.

Who ſhall ty the bell about the cats necke how,
Not I (quoth the mouſe) for a thing that I know.

Of had I wyſt. 256.

Beware of had I wyſt wyfe. Oh man tys to late
To beware therof ſyns thou were my wedded mate.

Of daunſyng. 257.

He dauncth attendance. are attendantes daunſyng?
Then haue we much daunſyng with ſmall auaunſyng.

Of the cat eatyng fyſhe. 258.

The cat woulde eate fyſhe but ſhe wyll not weate hir féete,
She thinkth fleſhe with dry féete more ſwéete thē fiſh w̄ wéete.

Of the blinde. 259.

The blynde eate many a flie, that we fynde,
Chefly where caruers to the blynde are blynde.

Of the woorſt and beſt. 260.

Prouyde for the woorſt, the beſt wyll ſaue it ſelfe.
For that ſauyng ſyde thou art a ſuttle elfe.

Of

Of all kyndis of thyngis thou haft prouifhin preft,
For thy neighbours the wurft, for thy felfe the beft.

Of fyue egges. 261.

He cumth in with his. v. egges, what egges to call?
Hen egges, goofe egges, or ducke egges, nay dawes egges all.

Of clymyng. 262.

He that neuer clymbd neuer fell, fum men clyme
For douys nefts and fynde dawes nefts fum tyme.

Of the wey. 263.

It is out of my way, fo it lyghtly may,
To all good thyngis thy way is out of the way.

Of waytyng. 264.

He wayteth for moone fhyne in the water,
Such waytyng fuch wynnyng thats a méete mater.

Of Ryme. 265.

It may ryme but it acordth not. cordth not Wyll,
Beware of cording rymes thofe rymes agrée yll.

Of fyfhyng. 266.

It is yll fyfhyng before the net.
Wurfe fyfhyng behynde as nets are fet.

Of good. 267.

He knowth none ende of his good, marke his wynnyng,
He knowth of his good none ende, nor begynnyng.

Of the hot yron. 268.

When the Iron is hot ftryke, ftryke hot Iron and ftéele,
But golde or fyluer to ftryke we haue no déele.

Of the purfe. 269.

Thy purfe is thréede bare, we fée on the out fyde,
And more bare on the in fyde when both fydes are tryde.

Of many handes. 270.

Many handes make lyght warke, many handes ye marke.
Ye muft fay thus. many lyght handes make lyght warke.

Otherwyfe.

Many hands make light woorke, no woorke is finde thée,
Thou canft not woorke thy hands be bounde behynde thée.

Of the lothe ſtake. 271.

The loth ſtake ſtandth longe, we haue many lothe ſtakes,
Eche ſtake welny to other it ſelfe, lothe makes.

Otherwyſe.

The lothe ſtake ſtandth longe, in ſome place, but ſome hande
Pluckth vp all ſtakes, ſuffrynge no ſtake longe to ſtande.

Of hauinge. 272.

Better to haue then wiſhe, nay ye may ſo craue,
That better to wyſhe ten tymes then once to haue.

Otherwyſe.

Better to haue then wyſhe, not alway coſyn,
What yf ye raſhely wyſht ſtrypes nowe a doſyn.

Otherwyſe.

Better to haue then wiſhe. better haue as we haue,
Then to haue at wiſhe all that wiſhers wolde craue.

Of counſell. 273.

Thrée may kepe councell if twayne be away.
But one foole doth ofte his owne councell bewray.

Otherwyſe.

Thrée may kepe councell if twayne be away,
Sum women I here ſay, that ſaiyng denay.

Of Roome. 274.

Roome was not bylt on one day, that is well knowne,
Nor in one day Rome wyll not be ouerthrowne.
For where Roome ſemd puld downe in one day brother,
There is Roome ſet vp agayne in an other.

Of Speeche. 275.

Spare to ſpeake ſpare to ſpéede.
Doome men wyn nought in déede,
And ſpéech as ſpéeche may fall
May wyn nought, and léeſe all.

Of one had in the wynde. 276.

I haue him in the wynde. wel ſyr it is your mynde
To haue him in the wynde, or hange him in the wynde.

Who

Of one yll ſhod. 277.

Who is woorſe ſhod then is the ſhomakers wyfe?
The deuyls wyfe, ſhe was neuer ſhod in hir lyfe.

Of all and naught. 278.

He woulde all haue and naught forgo, no,
He may all forgo and naught haue ſo,

Of warnyng. 279.

I gaue him ſcarborow warnyng, ſcarborow
That warnyng cam ſhort to bryng good harborow.

Of byrdes flowne. 280.

The byrdes are flowne, that byrdes neſt was yll watcht,
Byrdes wynges once full fumd byrdes wyll hardly be catcht.

Otherwyſe.

The byrds are flowne. Flowne, that flight no wunder brings
Byrds may ſone flée where byrders clyp no byrds wyngs.

Of leauyng. 281.

Leaue it or it leaue you, leaue what folly,
He can neuer leaue it nor it him wholly,

Of ſettyng in foote. 282.

He hath ſet in foote, thyngs by wyt to be ſped,
His foote ſhall dooe ſeruyce as good as his hed.

Otherwyſe.

I wyll ſet in foote, fréende thou maiſt ſet in fyt
Foote hand and hed but thou canſt ſet in no wyt.

Of faſt byndyng. 283.

Faſt bynd faſt fynd, nay thou weare prentyſe faſt bownde,
And yet ranſt thou a way where thou couldſt not be founde.

Of hap. 284.

Happy man happy dole, ſo ſay ſycke and hole,
But good hap is deintie, moſt men haue féeld good dole.

Otherwyſe.

Happy man happy dole, hap is full of holes,
Hap catcheth and holdeth very few good doles.

Y   Take

Of tyme. 285.

Take tyme when tyme cumth, we are oftymes told of it,
But when tyme cumth yet can we take no hold of it.

Otherwyfe.

Take tyme when tyme cumth, afay to be bolde of it,
But flyper as an eeles tayle is the holde of it.

Otherwyfe.

Take tyme when tyme cumth, are we fet tyme to take?
Beware tyme, in meane tyme, take not vs in brake,

Otherwyfe.

Take time when tyme cumth, when time cumth thou faift wel
But when cumth good tyme to take, I can not tell.

Of the fat hog. 286.

Euery man bafteth the fat hog. nay fréend nay,
Maft faylth fore this yere fat hogs pyne away.

Otherwyfe.

Euery man baftyth the fat hog, tis agréed
That thofe hogs fhall haue moft help that haue leaft néed.

The bale and boote. 287.

When bale is hekft, boote is next, though boote be nye
What helpyth boote, where bale is euer mofte hye.

Of fowes. 288.

As méete as a fowe to beare a faddle Ihon.
A fowe to beare a faddle, we haue féene none,
But though fowes beare no faddles yet may we fay
We fée faddles beare fowes welny euery day.

Of making a croffe. 289.

I wyll make a croffe vpon this gate, ye croffe on
Thy croffes be on gates all, in thy purfe non.

Of a pad. 290.

It wyll bréede a pad in the ftrawe, very wéele.
Beware it bréede not a padlocke on thy héele.

Of long ftandyng. 281.

Long ftandyng and fmall offryng makth poore parfons,
Long wayghtyng and fmall wages makth poore garfons.

Of the weaker.   292.

The weaker goth to the pot, ye, and god wot,
Sum the weaker for ofte goyng to the pot.

Of catchyng.   293.

Catch that catch may, after catchyng and fnatchyng,
Pyllyng and pollyng, we fall now to patchyng.

Of holdyng.   294.

Holde faft when ye haue it, if it be not thyne,
Holde faft and run faft when thou haft it fréend myne.

Of knowledge.   295.

I know him as well as the begger knowth his bag.
Thou knowft him, but when wilt thou know thy felfe wag.

Of fmellyngs.   296.

I fmeld him out, furder then he myght fmell thée.
The fmeller of fmellers then, thou art euyn he.

Of nought laide downe. '   297.

Nought lay downe nought take vp, welfayde,
Nought ly downe nought ryfe vp, welwayde.

Of fyght and fare.   298.

Ye fée your fare, a very ftraunge fare to fée.
A blynde man may fée our fare as well as wée.

Of the pot not broken.   299.

Neyther pot broken nor water fpylt, water
Thou fpylft none, but thou fpylft all other mater.

Of late and neuer.   300.

Better late then neuer. ye mate,
But as good neuer as to late.

Otherwyfe.

Better late then neuer.
That is not trew euer.
Sum thynges to rule in rate.
Better neuer then late.

FINIS.   Y ij

✠The fifth hundred of Epygrams.

Inuented and made by John Heywood.

LONDINI.
Anno Christi.
1 5 6 2.

To the reader.

Ere it as parellous to deale cardes at play,
As it is quarellous to deale bookes this day,
One and forty men, among one and fiftie,
Wolde flee one and thirtie, to flée one vnthriftie.
And yet Cardes fo dealt fhould haue, in reuealyng,
Foredeale of bookes in this harde time of dealyng.
Cardes be tooted on but on the tone fide:
Bookes on both fides : in all places porde and pride.
Not to content, but to contend, vpon fpiall
Of leaft tittle, that can come in triall.
If the best writer to write be much afrayde,
More may I (the woorft) by fearefull feare be ftayde.
And were not this one thing, feare fhould ftay me fo,
That booke or ballet, I neuer durft write mo.
In all my fimple writyng neuer ment I,
To touche any priuate perfon difpleafantly.
Nor none do I touche here : by name, but onely one,
Which is my felfe : whom I may be bolde vpon.
This ment in my makyng, fyns proofe doth declare,
I pray you readers to fcan this, by this fquare.
As I, for mirth, myrily did make it,
So you, in mirth, mirily will take it.

FINIS.

The Table.

FINIS.

The fifth hundred of Epigrammes.

Of weenyng and wottyng.   1.

Ise men in olde time, wold wéene thē selues fooles.
Fooles now in new time, wil wéene thē selues wise.
Wéene wise, and wot wise differ in wise schooles:
To wéene them selues wise, when fooles so deuise,
As foolishe as frutelesse, is thenterprise.
This case is thus adiudgde, in wisedomes schoole:
Who wéenth him self wise, wisdome wotth him a foole.
Made by Iohn Heywood to these fooles euerychone,
And made of Iohn Heywood, when he wéenth him selfe none.

Of a man of law and his clientes.   2.

Twentie clientes to one man of lawe,
For counsell in twentie matters did drawe.
Eche one praiyng at one instant to spéede,
As all at once woulde haue spéede to procéede.
Fréendes all (quoth the learned man) ile speake with none,
Till one barber haue shauen all, one by one.
To a barber they went all together:
And beyng shauen, they returnde agayne thyther.
Ye haue (quoth the lawier) tarid longe hence.
Sir (quoth one) twentie could not be shauen sence
Of one barber, for ye well vnderstande,
One barber can haue but one shauyng hande.
Nor one lawier (quoth he) but one talkyng tung
Learne clientis this lesson of this lawier sprung.
Like as the barber, one after one must shaue,
So clientes of counsailours, counsaile must haue.

An aduise agaynst mockyng.   3.

Vse to thy true fréende no derision
If thy fréende spie it, he takth it poyson.
Though thy fréend dissemble thespiall cléerely,
Yet spide in a fréende it toucheth him néerely.

Z   Telling

Tellyng thy fréende his faute, mockyng him not,
If he thanke thée not, then is he a fot.

Of itchyng and fmartyng.   4.

Itching and fmartyng, both touch vs at quicke.
When we itche, we fcratch : when we fmart, we kicke.
But in our kickyng at our prefent fmarte,
Let vs confider our former defarte.

Of a fharpe tunge.   5.

Wife, I perceiue thy tunge was made at Egeware.
Ye fir, and yours made at Rayly, harde by thare.

Of a horfe.   6.

A Tilt horfe, *alias* a beere horfe to bee,
Which wouldft thou bée ? a béere horfe I fay to thée.
When the horfe is féene chéerely to drawe the béere.
He is fo prayfde, that he may be proude to héere.
At Tilte when the horfe runthe as faft as he can,
All crie well runne, not to the horfe, to the man.
And if the horfe fall with the man ouerlade,
Then crie they all, a vengeance on that lame iade.

Of a butler and a hors.   7.

The butler and the béere horfe both be like one.
They drawe béere both : that is truth to bide one.
Bothe drawe béere in déede, but yet they differ Ione :
The butler drawth and drinkth béere, the horfe drinkth none.

Of braffe.   8.

I perceiue well now that braffe is waxen proude,
Becaufe braffe fo much with filuer is aloude.
And beyng both ioynde, fins they moft by braffe ftande,
That makth braffe bolde, to ftande on the vpper hande.

Of a louces dwellyng place.   9.

Were thou a louce and fhouldft choofe one dwellyng place,
Whether woldft thou dwell, hauing choife in this cafe,
In mens bigge breeches, or in womens thicke ruffes ?
I would be, both for the places and ftuffes,

                 In

In fommer with women, in winter with men.
In fommer the womans necke pleafant then,
In winter the mans bréeche is clofe and warme.
Large walks for life to walke warme without harme.
Galeries, gable endes, cambers, parlers, halles,
Colde froft to defende, a dofen double walles.
Som féeld, fom hangd, fom dide, fom painted, fom ftaind,
Rents of all fife, great and fmall rentes retaynd.
And when by louce bityng, the legge is itchyng,
The barres of mens breeches haue fuch ftrōg ftitching,
Such bolftring, fuch broydring, let men ftare and ftampe,
The louce is as fafe there, as he were in a campe.
In winter I fay thefe breeches are alone.
But then in fommer let the louce thens be gone,
For feare of a plague : if he then thither gette,
A thoufande to one, he fhall die of the fwette.

Of a ftraunge glaffe. 10.

Good god what a glaffe to vewe is this?
See what an vnfightly fight here is.
Great promife, fmall performance.
Great countenaunce, fmall continuance.
Great winnyng, fmall fauyng.
Great hopyng, fmall hauyng.
Great hiues, fmall hony.
Great purfes, fmall mony.
Great gappes, fmall bufhes.
Great fpeares, fmall pufhes.
Great wine, fmall water.
Great woordis, fmall mater.
Great botome, fmall brinke.
Great brewyng, fmall drinke.
Great rent, fmall place.
Great fpace, fmall grace.

Z ij   Great

Great drift, fmall fhifte.
Great gift, fmall thrifte.
Great watchyng, fmall catchyng.
Great patchyng, fmall matchyng.
Great bloud, fmall bruite.
Great flowers, fmall fruite.
Great wooddes, fmall okes.
Great ftaues, fmall ftrokes.
Great hennes, fmall egges.
Great hofe, fmall legges.
Great ftudie, fmall arte.
Great defyre, fmall defarte.
Great geuyng, fmall takyng.
Great marryng, fmall makyng.
Great fhippes, fmall faylyng.
Great loffe, fmall auaylyng.
Great markyng, fmall myndyng.
Great feekyng, fmall findyng.
Great lawyng, fmall louyng.
Great fturryng, fmall mouyng.
Great fowyng, fmall growyng.
Great trowyng, fmall knowyng.
I trow fo great ill, and fo fmall good,
In one glaffe together, neuer ftood.

Of driuyng and drawyng. 11.

If thou muft be forfte foorth to take iorney quicke,
Whether woldft thou be driuen forth, or drawne forth Dicke?
I wolde be driuen forth Iacke : for as doth appéere,
Drawyng and hangyng drawe vengeable néere.
I thynke it leffe ill Iacke, hauyng choyfe in fcope.
To be driuen with the whip, then drawne to the rope.

Of longe futes. 12.

Sutes hange halfe a yere in Weftminfter hall,
At Tyburne, halfe an houres hangyng endeth al.

Nothyng

Of lightneſſe.   13.

Nothyng is lighter then a feather, Kytte,
Yes climme : what light thing is that ? thy light wytte.

Of a diſagreement.   14.

Eche one man welny falth out with an other,
And lykewyſe eche thynge diſagreeth with other.
Namely malte and water, theſe two thinges are
So far falne a funder, by ſcornefull ſquare,
That no bruer, be he luſtie or lither,
Dare couch malte and water, in houſe togyther.
But chiefly ſowre water now beareth ſuch ſway,
That, ſwéete malte from brewhouſe, water driuth away.

Of chepenyng of conies.   15.

Iane thou felleſt ſwéete conies in this pultry ſhoppe :
But none ſo ſwéete as thy felfe, ſwéete conye moppe.
What is the price of thée ? forſooth ſhe tolde,
At what pryce ſo euer my felfe ſhalbe ſolde,
Strange is the hearyng, for ware or for monye,
To heare a woodcocke cheapen a conye.

Of a wyfe hauyng childe.   16.

My wyfe hath a childe now at fowre ſcore and ten.
At fowre ſcore and ten yeres ? nay fréend, nay : what then ?
At fowre ſcore and ten quarters of a yere I ment.
Ment ye ſo ? and I ment yeres. by which extent
Your wyfe might féeme your mother : but now I ſmell,
You may féeme your wyues father wonderfoole well.

Of a bachiler and a mayde.   17.

Is that bachiler a wooer to that mayde ?
The commons common ſo : tys commonly ſayde.
Where dwelth that bachiler ? wyde a bowe of brydewell.
Where dwelth that mayde ? at broken wharfe very well.

Of ſhorte payment.   18.

Thy dettar wyll paie thée ſhortly : ſhortly ?
He will make that ſhort lye, a longe lye, dread I.

Z iij   Whence

Whence certaine thinges came fyrſt. 19.

Whens come great breeches? from little wittam.
Whens come great ruffes? from ſmall brainfoorth they cam.
Whens come theſe round verdingales? from ſquare thrift.
Whens come deepe copped hattes? from ſhallow ſhift.
Whens come braudered gardis? from the towne of euill.
Whens come vncomde ſtaryng heades? from the deuill.
Whens come theſe womans ſcarfs? from folly Iohn.
Whens come their glitteryng ſpanges? from much wanton.
Whens come perfumde gloues? from curioſitee.
Whens come fyne trapt moyles? from ſuperfluitee.
Whens come cornde crooked toes? from ſhort ſhapen ſhoone.
Whens come wylde hie lookers? from midſomer moone.
Whens come fayre painted faces? from peinters tooles.
Whens come all theſe? from the vicar of ſainct fooles.

Of furred and lyned gownes. 20.

Thicke furd gownes worne in ſōmer, ſhew bare worn thréedis.
Thin linde gownes worne in winter, come from S. néedes.

Of a wyne drawer. 21.

Drawer, thy wyne is euen with thée now I ſée:
Thou perſyſte the wyne, and the wyne perſeth thée.

Shorte checkes betwene a man and his wyfe. 22.

I am carefull to ſée thee careleſſe, Iyll:
I am wofull to ſée thee wytleſſe, Wyll.
I am anguiſhte to ſée thee an ape, Iyll:
I am angry to ſée thee an aſſe, Wyll.
I am frettyng to ſée thee flee from me, Iyll:
I am ſory to ſée thee feeke to me, Wyll.
I am madde to ſée the mate thy huſbande, Iyll:
I am ſad to ſée thee ſklaunder thy wyfe, Wyll.
I am dumpyſhe to ſée thee play the drabbe, Iyll:
I am knappyſhe to ſée the plaie the knaue, Wyll.

My

Of a woman deckt in two coloures. 23.

My honny bes, blacke and white doth fet the out nette.
Thy here whyte as perle, thy téeth blacke as iette.

Of vnfweete breath. 24.

Thine vnfauery breath lackth falte, beale belfabubbe :
It hath tane to much wynde in the poudryng tubbe.
Thy breath, hodge, with falte is fo fauery to fmell,
That no feafonyng lyckour, can feafon it well.

Of clyppyng and clenfyng. 25.

Not clyppyng your beards, why clyp you your nayles ?
Not kombyng your heades, why wype you your tayles ?
Thefe beyng fuperfluous thinges euery chone,
Kombe, clip, or clenfe all : or clip or clenfe none.

Of a man and his wyues departyng. 26.

Wife I will go abrode. wyll ye take the payne ?
Beete : but when the diuell will ye come in agayne ?
Makft thou me a diuell ? nay then be out of dout,
The diuell will come in, when the diuels damme goth out.

An account of a mans children. 27.

Wyfe, of ten babes betwene vs by encreafe growne,
Thou faift I haue but nyne . no mo of your owne.
Of all thynges encrefyng, as my confcience lythe,
The parfon muft needes haue the tenth for the tythe.

Of a woman of Huntington. 28.

Where dwelft thou Sys ? I dwell at huntington nowe.
Lyke fo, for thou lookft lyke a nowe hunted fowe.
Where dwelft thou Sym ? at hammer fmith dwell I.
A meete foyle for thee ? for hammer hed is hard by.

Of a laundres. 29.

A lyke laundres to thee, neuer fawe I.
Thy clothes wafht but once a weeke commonly,
Thy felfe wafhte once in an houre vfually.
And yet eche weekes ende doth this thus trie,
Thy clothes euer wette, thy felfe euer drie.

This

Of a cutter of purſlane.

This herbe purſlane thou cutſt pretily I ſée:
But to cut apurſe in a lane, none lyke thée.

Of one ſtandyng in his owne conceite. 31.

He ſtandth well in his owne conceyte eche man tels.
So had he néede, for he ſtandth in no mans els.

Of one that hard without eares. 32.

I ſée men heare, though they eares haue none.
Thou doſte heare me ſpeake, thine eares beyng gone.

Of an archers rouyng. 33.

What a ſhafte ſhootes he with a rouyng arrowe?
Styll he hyts the marke, be it wyde or narrowe.
Where ſhooteth this ſharpe ſhootyng archer moſt, Wyll?
He ſhooteth moſt at rouers on ſhooters hyll.

Of perill to one by the number of three. 34.

In thy hand I ſée, thy fortune ſhalbe ſuche,
That the numbre of thrée ſhall daunger the muche.
Thrée bedfelowes in thy bed ſhall diſpleaſe thée,
Thrée lice in thy bumme bréeche ſhall ofte diſeaſe thée,
Three cuppes full at once ſhall oft dyſgyſe thée,
Three bearers of the hom ſhall ofte diſpiſe thée
Thrée drinkes, wyne, ale, and beere, ſhall ouerflowe thée,
Three wreſtlers in one ſygne ſhall ouerthrowe thée,
Three wiues in thrée yeres ſhall wonderſly weare thée,
Three ſhe beares thoſe three yeres, ſhall al to teare thee.
But in thinges numbred by three, aboue all théeſe,
Blis the three thouſand tymes, from frame of three tréeſe.

Of gloria patri. 35.

Dicke I meruaile muche, why in eury plat,
Gloria paitri ſtandth before *Sicut erat.*
Tom, *Gloria patri* is a gentleman:
In pleaſant ſpéeche, ſpeake ſo ſweetely no tung can.
Sicut erat is a churle ſo rude and playne,
That to here him ſpeake, all degrees do diſdaine.

Is

Of a dyar. 36.

Is thy huſband a dyar woman ? alacke,
Had he no colour to die the on but blacke ?
Dieth he oft ? ye, to oft when cuſtomers call,
But I wolde haue him one day, die once for all.
Were he gone, diar woulde I neuer mo wed,
Diars be euer diyng, but neuer ded.

Of a Iugge. 37.

Pot him Iacke : pot him Iacke ? nay pot him Iugge.
To pot the drunkarde, the Iugge is the dugge.

Of the three cuppes. 38.

Whers thine In Iohn ? at thrée cuppes in bredſtrete Ihone.
At thrée cuppes in breadſtrete ? well let bread alone.
At thoſe thrée cuppes when euer thou dines or ſuppes,
Ere thou goe to bed, thou haſt in all thy cuppes.

Of braſſe and Iron. 39.

Braſſe and olde Iron who brought thoſe two togyther ?
Braſſe thinketh ſcorne to ſée them brought ſo hyther.
Olde Iron is rouſty and rotten to vewe,
Braſſe with ſyluer fayre blauncht and polyſhte newe.

Otherwyſe.

Braſſe ſaide to olde Iron with braſſe perkyng late,
Backe ye kancred karle, ye be not my mate.
Backe braſſe (quoth Iron) plainnes is moſt talowe.
I ſhewe as I am : and ſo doſt not thou.

Of Iacke and Iohn. 40.

Iacke and Iohn in degrée dyffer farre brother.
Iacke dawe is one, maſter Iohn dawes is an other.

Of wreſtlyng. 40.

Where we wreſtled by couples, we wreſtle alone:
And ſhall, tyll tyme our ſhakled bréeches be gone.
In ſteppyng and ſtrydyng it is a wunder,
How we wreſtle to get our legges a funder.

Aa   If

Of pryde. 42.

If thou wil néedes be proud, marke this fréend myne:
Of good déedes be not proude : they are not thyne.
But when thou plaieſt the knaue in yll déedes growne,
Be proud of thoſe yll déedes : they are thyne owne.

Of one hanged. 43.

What faute had he done that was hangde yeſterday?
Of any faute done by him I can nought ſay.
Two or thrée two peny tryfles were layd to him,
But, his fayre gay hangde houſe, man, did vndo hym,
Here is tyt for tat, meaſure met very trym:
Firſt he hangd his houſe, now his houſe hath hangd him.

Of a dettar. 44.

Doth your maſterſhyppe remember your dette to mée?
Remember my dette? ye fréende, I warrant thée:
I remember it ſo, that though I ſay it,
Ile neuer forget it, nor neuer pay it.

Of louinge of a gooſe. 45.

A gooſe, gréene or gray whiche loueſt thou better?
A gréene gooſe : for it is farre the ſwetter.
Loue both as thy ſelfe, for as proofe ſhewth ryfe,
Thou art and haſt béene a gooſe, all thy lyfe.

Otherwyſe.

Thou loueſt a gooſe to much : ware ſurfet elfe.
I neuer ſawe gooſe yet, lyke thée, loue him ſelfe.

Of harpe ſtringes. 46.

Which ſtring in all the harpe wouldſt thou ſtyll harpe on.
Not the baſe, I will be none vnderlyng, Iohn.
Nor the ſtandyng tennor : for ſtiffe ſtandyng.
Nor the treble : for feare of to hye hangyng.
Nor the counter tennor : for countryng to long.
Vpon what harpe ſtryng then wouldſt thou harpe thy ſong?
Aboue all ſtryngs, when we ſhall fall to harpyng.
The harp ſtryng to harp on, is the meane harp ſtryng.

Take

Of fortune. 47.

Take thy fortune as it falth, fome aduifeth:
But I wolde fayne take fortune as it rifeth.

Of choyce. 48.

Choice is good in moft thingis folke fay, in which choife,
For choife of one of two thinges, thou maift reioice:
For man aliue lyke thee franke choyfe can haue,
To play the knauyfhe foole, or the foolyfhe knaue.

Of a falfe bragge. 49.

I was neuer but an honeft man.
Put out that but, and thou faift truth than.

Of liyng and true faiyng. 50.

Wyfe, the people are difpofed all to lye:
For thou art commended vnyuerfallye.
Nay fyr : the people to tell truth, are all bolde,
For you are difcommended of younge and olde.

Of a dawe pate. 51.

Thou arte a very dawe pate, as euer I fawe.
Sir, in déede the pate is chiefe parte of a dawe:
For when dawes fhall appere in any cofte,
For all thofe dawes parts, their dawe pates be mofte.

Of water and wyne. 52.

Thou makft curtfy to wafhe handis with water of mine.
Makyng no curtfy to wafhe thy mouth with my wine.
But I pray the make this change in this matter?
More curtfy at my wyne, and leffe at my water.

Betwene dogges and a deere. 53.

Set malles afyde : fayde a bucke to a greyhounde.
Beware of pryde : faid that dogge to that déere.
Be pacient in trouble : a hounde fayde rounde,
Louyng aduyfe to this déere this dyd appeere.
In which counfell geuen, to kyll him they run neere.
Whiche counfayle amounth to this euery man féeth,
Comfort him with their tunges, kyll him with their téeth.

Aa ij   It

Of twelue and one.   54.

It is twelue a clocke : fyr tys more, well ny one.
Is one more then twelue ? thats a reafon alone.
Sir when the daie to after noone dooth amounte,
One is more then twelue, by our fextens accounte.

Of verdingales.   55.

Alas poore verdingales muft lie in the ftreete :
To houfe them, no doore in the citee made meete.
Syns at our narow doores they in can not win,
Send them to Oxforde, at Brodegates to get in.

Preceptes of a man to his wyfe.   56.

Stande ftyll wyfe, I wyll :
Be ftill wyfe, I nyll.
Now barke wyfe, I wyll :
To warke wyfe, I nyll.
Proue me wyfe, I wyll :
Loue me wyfe, I nyll.
Now chat wyfe, I wyll :
Leaue that wyfe, I nyll.
Keepe chayre wyfe, I wyll :
Speake fayre wyfe, I nyll.

Of an expert man.   57:

Is he fuch an expert man ? an expert man ?
Put out that ex, and no man more expert than.

Of deliuerance from yll.   58.

Wyfe, from all euyll, when fhalt thou deliuered bee ?
Sir, when I (faid fhe) fhalbe deliuered from thée.

Of cuttyng of the herbe tyme.

All tymes of the day to night from the pryme,
Thou gardner wylte not leaue cuttyng of tyme.
Thou wylt neuer leaue cuttyng of tyme, I fee,
Tyll fuche tyme, as tyme, fhall in tyme cutte of thee.

Sweatyng

Of one fearyng the ſwette. 60.

Sweatyng ſicknes ſo fearſt thou beyonde the marke,
That winter or ſommer thou neuer ſweatſt at warke.

Of one thinkyng on an other. 61.

When doth your maiſterſhip thinke on me? euer.
When do you thinke vpon my matter? neuer.
Me ye remember, my matter ye forget:
Remembrance and forgetfulneſſe, is wrong ſet.
For I wolde wiſhe you rather, if it might bée,
To remember my matter, and forget mée.

Of one beyng at a poynt. 62.

Is he at a poynte with his creditors? yée.
For he is not woorth a pointe they all ſée.

Of teſtons. 63.

Teſtons be gone to Oxforde, god be their ſpéede:
To ſtudie in Brazennoſe there to procéede.

Of redde Teſtons. 64.

Theſe Teſtons looke redde: how like you the ſame?
Tis a token of grace: they bluſhe for ſhame.

Of ſtampyng. 65.

We ſtampe crabs, we ſtamp teſtons: which ſtamping doone
We ſtare vppon Teſtons now beyond the moone.
Which ſtampyng of Teſtons brought it not ſome ſkill,
Our ſtaryng on Teſtons could iudge them but ill.
But as the whot ſunne melteth ſnowe away,
So ſhall whotte fire melt colde Teſtons, as folke ſay.
We, for Teſtons leauyng ſcoldyng and ſquaryng.
And on Teſtons leauyng ſtampyng and ſtaryng.

Of Iohn longe the carier.

Of what length is Iohn long the carier Prat?
A quarter of a yere long. how proueſt thou that?
Thertéene wéekes paſt he ſhuld haue brought me a wat:
But yet long Iohn, Iohn long: with that wat comth nat.

Aa iij   Where-

189

Wherby I Iohn ſhort, am as ſhort to compare,
As Iohn longe by this length is long to declare.
For as Iohn long lurkth to long this wat to fet,
So I Iohn ſhort leape to ſhort this wat to get.

Of turnyng. 67.

Wilt thou vſe turners craft ſtill? ye by my trouth.
Much thrift and moſt ſuretie in turners craft growth.
Halfe turne or whole turne, where turners be turning,
Turnyng kéepes turners from hangyng and burning.

Of maſter Carter. 68.

Is that gentlemans name maſter Carter? ye.
How his name and condicions differ now ſe.
So cunnyng, ſo cumly, ſo curteiſie, ſo kinde,
So gentle a gentleman in eche mans minde:
That all men are ſtriken in pitifull wunder,
To ſée maſter carter and the carte a ſunder.

Of goyng farre. 69.

As he goth farre that neuer doth turne him backe,
So goſte thou farre wide : thou neuer turnſt againe.
Wher thou goeſt, or what thou doſte, come luck come lacke,
Thy ſelfe or thy matters foorth they go amaine.
To turne againe no counſayle can thée ſtrayne.
Except thy will ſhall ſhowe thy witte in the wane,
Finde meanes to take a houſe in turne againe lane.

How money is made lame. 70.

Money, with couetouſneſſe thou doſt reſt ſo,
That lacke of vſe doth lame thée : thou canſt not go.
With prodigalitée thou trudgeſt ſo faſt,
That exceſſe of to much exerciſe, doth lame thée at laſt,
Theſe twoo beyng lame lettis of extremitées,
Where woldſt thou be lotted to be from both thées ?
With liberalitée wolde I be the meane.
With liberalitée ? nay he is gone cleane.

Lady

Of an olde woer. 71.

Lady I loue you, in way you to wed:
But mine age with your youth difagréeth fo,
That if I fpeake: I thinke not to be fped.
Your age in your fute, is no whit your fo,
To your yeres many, had ye many mo.
We wold wed the fooner by yeres, fhowyng plaine,
That I fhould the fooner be vnwed againe.

Of a yong wooer. 72.

I brought thée late an olde riche widow to woo:
Whom thou mightft haue had, but nought woldft thou thē doo
Nor nought canft thou do now: thrift and thou art od.
For now lieth fhe fpéechles at mercy of god.
For the mercy of god bring me now to hir:
I neuer fawe méete time: till now, to woo hir.

Of weakeneffe and ftrength. 73.

Weakenes and ftrength, here fhowft thou both in préefe,
Thou art a weake man, and yet a ftrong théefe.

Warnyng of pride. 74.

Beware of pride, fayft thou to mée?
Let pride, fay I, beware of thée.
In euery place thou dooft fo watche him,
That if pride fturre, thou wilt fure catche him.

Of pacience. 75.

Be pacient in trouble. how can that bée?
Sins out of trouble nothyng pleafeth thée.

Of pleafyng. 76.

Be glad to pleafe, yea be glad to pleafe brother.
But whom? pleafe thy felfe, fée thou pleafe none other.

Of a hande gonne and a hande. 77.

Thou haft a good handgoonne: but whats thy hand?
When thou fhootft of, out of daunger to ftand,
No ftandyng more fure in any place or plat,
Then to ftande clofe to the marke thou fhootft at.

Braffe

Of braſſe and ſiluer.　78.

Braſſe hath béene a loft, with ſiluer ſet vp.
Come downe braſſe and drinke on an aſhen cup.

Of difference betwene wiſe men aud fooles.　79.

Betwéene wiſe men and fooles, among thinges many
This one differth . when both ſortes get things any.
Which to their pleaſures are pleaſantly alloud,
Of thoſe thingis wun, wiſe mē are glad, fooles be proud.

Of a pithy witte.　80.

Good god, what a pithy wit haſt thou Dicke?
The pith of thy woordes ſo déepe and ſo tricke,
Thy woordes ſo pythily pearſe to the quicke,
Pith of no woordes agaynſt thy woordes may kicke,
No more then the pith of a goonſtone may pricke,
Againſt the pithy pith of an elder ſticke.

Of choiſe to be a wiſe man or a foole.　81.

A wyſe man or a foole : if thou muſt be one,
Which woldſt thou be in winter, Iohn? a foole Ihone.
Where beſt men in winter ſit next fire from colde,
There ſtandis the foole warme while all his tales be tolde.
Which woldſt thou be in ſommer, when winter is gon?
A foole. a foole, why? that why ſhowth herevpon.
In ſommer when ſtates ſit from fire in the coole,
At that boordes ende in coole ayre there ſtands the foole.
Winter and ſommer what time men muſt to wurke,
Which woldſt thou be? a foole to looke on and lurke.
All times of the yere for one thing or other,
Better be a foole then a wiſe man brother.

Of a knightes carterly coller.　82.

I bad this carter bring my collar of golde:
And he bringth me my horſe collar, holde knaue holde.
Sir if I may ſpeake my thought without fearyng,
This collar of both ſhowth beſt for your wearyng.

Of

Of males and male horſes.   83.

Of al horſe, a male horſe would I not bée.
Where he erſt bare one male, now berth he thrée.
Thoſe are one behinde and one on eche ſide,
The man, who on the male horſe doth ride,
Werth on eche legge, one male. for his ſloppes are,
Eche one ſloppe one male (kindely to declare.)
Longe, round, wyde, weightie as a male eche one.
But all horſe are now male horſes euerychone.
For euery one horſe, bearth twoo males at leaſte.
Of male horſe and male men, fréends heres a feaſte.

A man diſcommended.   84.

Not once a yere ought ſéene in thée to alowe.
Not once a yere thy knée to god dooſt thou bowe.
Not once a yere openeſt thou thy lippes to pray.
Not once a yere ſhowſte thou goodneſſe any way.
Not once a yere geueſt thou almes to the poore,
Not once a yere dooſt thou repent thée therfore.
But all times a yere thou wouldſt all vnderſtood.
Thou neuer dooſt repent, but when thou dooſt good.

Of runnyng.   85.

In pooſte haſte run hooreſon run. art thou here yet?
Shall I run out of breath? nay run out of thy wit.

Of polling.   86.

Our heads grow to long, god geue our barbers curſes.
Our barbers polle no heads, our barbers polle purſes.

Of plate lente forth.   87.

Where is thy plate? lent out to a mariage.
Whither? to ſainct néedis . to whom? to maſter gage.

Of a man of law and his wife.   88.

You beyng a pleader at law exelente,
Yet hath your wife brought you to an exigent.
Pray hir to let fall thaction at law now,
Or els, ſo god helpe me, ſhe will ouerlaw yow.

Bb   Pennes

Of pennes and pence. 89.

Pennes and pence, differ far in proporcion.
The penny flat and round, the pen ftraight and long.
And yet for aydes, in cafe of extorcion,
Pennes and pence are like in workyng of wrong.

Of a womans thinne tounge. 90.

I neuer faw wife like thine for this thyng : Dicke,
Hir tung woondrous thin, and hir fpéech wondrous thicke.
Tom, I haue fpent much in vaine fince fhe was yong,
To haue hir thicke fpéeche as thinne as hir tong.
It is the tunge of tunges : Dicke, for runnyng rounde :
I take the tippe for filuer : by the fhrill founde.
It hath Tom, a fhakyng fharpe founde in the eare.
But it is no filuer, wolde god it weare.

Of drinkyng to a man. 91.

I drinke to thée Iohn : nay thou drinkft frō me Ihone.
When thou drinkft to me, drinke for me thou leueft none.

Of runnyng at Tilte. 92.

We apply the fpigot, till tubbe ftande a tilte.
Ye, ren at the fpigot tilt, leaue the fpeare tilte thou wilte.

Of expence. 93.

What may he fpend ? ten pound a yere he might fpend.
Ift morgagde ? nay : no man will one peny lende
Vpon it . ift folde ? nay, no man will bie it.
Then he holdth it : nay, he can not come nie it.
Why foole ? how may he fpend ten pound by year than ?
I faid not he may, but he might fpende it man.
Meanyng he might fpend it, if he had it.
O, if he had it : a fir the diuell mad it.

Of fraying of babes. 94.

When do mothers fray their babes moft from duggis.
When they put on blacke fcrafs, and go like beare buggis.

Wyl

Of Reedes and Okes.   95.

Wyll you réedes at the windis will ftil make lowe beckis?
Wyll you Okes ftand ftiffe ftil while wind breke your neckis?
Wyll you reedes, like apes, ftill tucke & bowe eche ioynt?
Wyll you okes, like affes, ftill ftand ftiffe at one point?
Wyll you réedes be ftill bendyng bowyng bodies?
Wyll you okes be ftill ftoute ftiffe necked nodies?
Wyll you réedes be ftaggeryng ftill for vayne auayles?
Wyll you okes be ftern ftill till your tops kiffe your tayles?
Wyll you reedes fhrinke ftill to all windes towardly?
Wyll you okes fwell ftill at all windes frowardly?
Wyll you réedes crouch ftill to be the windis footeftooles?
Wyll you okes crake ftill to be the windis hed fooles?
Okes wyll doo as we haue.doone. fo wyll we réedes.
Wherin for our purpofe marke what ende procéedes.
In eche one ftorme a thoufand okes downe are blowne
In a thoufand ftormes not one réede ouerthrowne.

Of biyng a morter.   96.

That fpice mortar to fell it be you willyng?
Yea miftres? whats the price? ten fhillyng.
Ten fhillyng? freende: I am hither entifed
To bie a fpice morter, not a morter fpifed.

Of a ftepmother.   97.

Thy fathers fecond wife, thy fteppe mother,
For a fteppe mother thers not fuch an other.
At three fteppes I faw hir fteppe, fins fhe was wed,
From a ftayre foote, ftraight vp to thy fathers hed.

Of a lyar.   98.

Where doth Frances fabler now lie, Iane?
At figne of the whetftone in double tunge lane.
He lieth by night: and by day dayly hée
Lieth downe right, in what place fo euer he bée.
That he lieth ftill day and night, this thing doth trie,
He neuer fpeketh woorde but it is a lie.

Cc ij   One

Of tunges and pinſons. 99.

One difference this is, on which our tunges may carpe,
Betwéene pinching pinſons, and tauntyng tunges ſharpe.
Where theſe twoo nippers nip any were or when,
Thoſe pinſons nip dead thingis, thoſe tunges nip quick men.

Of Heywood. 100.

Art thou Heywood with the mad mery wit?
Ye forſooth maiſter, that ſame is euen hit.
Art thou Heywood that applieth mirth more then thrift?
Ye ſir, I take mery mirth a golden gift.
Art thou Heywood that hath made many mad plaies?
Ye many plaies, fewe good woorkes in all my daies.
Art thou Heywood that hath made men mery long?
Ye: and will, if I be made mery among.
Art thou Heywood that woulde be made mery now?
Ye ſir: helpe me to it now I beſeche yow.

FINIS.

A sixt hundred of Epi=grammes.

Newly inuented and made by John Heywood.

♣

LONDINI.
Anno Chriſti.
1 5 6 2.

To the reader.

Reeaders, reade this thus : for Preface, Proface.
Much good do it you : the poore repaſt here,
A ſyxt hundred dyſhes I bryng in place
To make good welfare, nay to make good chéere.
Fare is foode : chéere is mirth : ſins meate is déere,
Not of meate but of myrth, cum yong cum olde,
Cum who cum wyll, here is open houſholde.

FINIS.

The Table.

FINIS.

Of Rebellion. 1.

Gainft god I dayly offend by frailte:
But againft my prince, or natiue countre,
With as much as bodkin, when I rebell,
The next daie after hang me vp faire and well.
The next daie after? nay the next daie before
Wifhe thou thy felfe hangd, in that case euermore.
Before, thou hangft honeftly vnwoorthyly.
After, thou hangft, woorthyly vnhoneftly.
But ho? at our fyrft dyfhe in our mery feaft,
Why talke we of hangyng our myrth to moleft.
Be our chéefe no better then our pottage is,
Better faft than feaft at fuch feaftes as is this.
But beyng true to god, quéene, countre, and crowne,
We fhall at all feaftes, not hang vp, but fyt downe.

Otherwyfe.

Wylt thou be taken for a true Englyfhe man?
Ye : be true to god, thy quéene, and countre than.
Stand faft by thy countre, who euer wold wyn it,
Better ftand faft by it, then hang faft in it.

Of toung, mouth, teeth, and wifdome. 2.

The tounge is affinde, of woordes to be forter:
The mouth is affinde, to be the tounges dorter:
The téeth are affynde, to be the tounges porter:
But wifdome is fynde, to tye the tounge fhorter.

Of fyluer to be borowed. 3.

Haft thou any bowde fyluer to lende me Ione?
Nay : haft thou any broken fyluer for me? none.
Haft thou any clypt fyluer? I had, but tis gone.
Haft thou any crakt grote? crakt grote? nay not one.
No fyluer, bowde, broken, clypt, crakt, nor cut,
Hers a fréend for fréendfhyp, not woorth a crakt nut.

Cc   This

Of an vnkyndly march.　4.

This lyke marche, as lyke as I am a march hare.
March is not fo lyke marche fréend: I would it ware.
Though fhap of the March hare fhow not in thee,
Yet haft thou the marche hares mad propertee.

Of goyng to heauen and hell.　5.

Of heauen or of hell, which go folke faftest to?
To hell foole to hell, go fer more faft they do.
The hie way to both lyth thus as clarks tell,
Vp hill to heauenward, downe hill to hell.

Of the high way and a maydes face.　6.

The more the highway is wafht, the fouler it is.
Mayde, the high way and thy face are lyke in this.

Of one that would be prayfed.　7.

Wouldft thou be praifed? ye: why? praife pleafeth mé well.
Ye, but how doth deferte of prayfe pleafe the, tell.

Of lookyng.　8.

Looke vpward to heauen my fréend: what, where lookft thou?
Sir, I was lookyng downeward to hell for you.

Of a hare a foote.　9.

I here by the hounds, the hare is a foote.
Then muft fhe to horfbacke, none other boote.
Nothyng doth more a hares hope of lyfe quayle,
Then doth a houndes nofe, ny a hares tayle.

Of Hob and Iohn.　10.

Horfe and harneffe vp, on all handis: Hob and Iohn.
Hob and Iohn? nay. Lob and Iohn: would now be gon.
But tyll your prince fturre you to harneffe to ftart:
Harneffe you your horfe, and get ye to the cart.

Of feekyng a daw.　11.

I haue fought fer to finde a daw: why thou elfe,
When thou wouldft quicly fynde a daw, féeke thy felfe.
What is Domine dawe in Englifhe to fay?
No mo Dawes: thou dawe, art dawes enowe for this day.

To

Of ſaiyng grace.   12.

To ſay grace fayre and to ſay grace oft Iohn,
From Gracechurch to Grantam, thy lyke thers non.
At breackfaſt, at diner, at ſupper, at all,
At ſyttyng, at ryſyng, haue grace we ſhall.
Thers no man a lyue, in houſe, ſtréete, or féelde,
That ſaith grace ſo ofte, and ſhowth grace ſo ſeelde.

Of Dette.   13.

What diffrence in true dette, and blew dette, to rate?
Diffrence as in diſtance Ludgate and Newgate.

Of ſtepping.   14.

In ſteppyng one foote backe, ſteppyng forward twayne,
My ſteps ſo ſtept, are not ſtept in vayne.
If one backſtep, be as much as foreſteps thrée,
By your ſtout ſteppyng your wynnyng let vs ſée.
Where wyde ſtrydyng ſteppyng gets no gayne ought woorth,
As good to ſtand ſtone ſtyll, as ſtep one ſtep foorth.

Of wrytyng a gentleman.   15.

Thou writſt thy ſelfe gentleman in one woord brother.
But gentle is one woord, and man is a nother.

Of a wyues affection to hir huſband.   16.

I wene thers no wyfe lyke the wyfe of thyne.
Thy body beyng hers, yet dooth ſhe enclyne,
Fayreſt, or fouleſt, whom fancy doth prefer,
To take whom thou lyſt, ſo thou touche not her.

Of a mans thrift.   17.

Lorde what thrift aryſeth in thy behalfe?
Thy ſowe great with pyg, thy cowe great with calfe:
Thy ewe great with lambe: thy bytch great with whelpe:
Thy cat great with kytte: and more encreaſe to helpe,
Thy wyfe great with childe: and to ſhew thy thrift ſoole,
Thy mare great with fole, and thy ſelfe great with foole.

Cc ij   Thou

Of learnyng the lawe. 18.

Thou wilte lerne the lawe, where euer thou bée.

Lyncolnes In, or Lincolne towne, both one to thée.

Of good wyll and good deedes. 19.

Is good will the best part of a fréend ? nay, nay:

Beggers with lordis fo, for fréendfhyp compare may.

Good déedes by good wyll had, differ there brother.

A pooddyng pricke is one, a mylpoft is an other.

Of Newgate wyndowes. 20.

All Newgate wyndowes bay wyndowes they bée.

All lookers out there ftand at bay we fée.

Of treadyng a fhooe awrye. 21.

My wife doth euer tread hir fhooe a wry.

Inward, or outward ? nay, all outwardly:

She treadth fo outward, that if fhe out wyn,

She wyll by hir wyll, neuer treade foote within.

Of a fayre foowe. 22.

I neuer fawe a fayrer foowe in my lyfe.

A fyr, thy foowe is euen as faire as thy wyfe.

Of prayer. 23.

Some pray *familorum familarum.*

Sum fay, that is folorum, folarum.

Of cheefe. 24.

I neuer faw Banbery chéefe thicke enough:

But I haue oft féene Effex chéefe quicke enough.

Of a leafe. 25.

Thy leafe of frefhwharfe, byndth thée there to dwell:

Which thou haft forfyted, as thy neighbors tell:

Thefe foure yeres at frefhwharfe as folke confyther,

Thou haft not bene frefh, full foure houres togyther.

Of ftockes. 26.

Thy vpper ftocks be they ftufte with fylke or flocks,

Neuer become the lyke a nether payre of ftocks.

Wyfe,

A taunt of a wife to her husband. 27.

Wyfe, I wéene thou art dronke or Leunitike.
Nay hufband : women are neuer moone ficke.
Come that coniunction in time, late, or foone,
Wée fay (not the woman) the man in the moone.

Of pride. 28.

Fie on pride when men go nakte : nakte or clothed,
Pride is in all men a thyng to be lothed.
But yet may ye fée, though it doo ill acorde,
Sum nakte begger as proude, as fome clothed lorde.

To walke, talke, drinke or fleape. 29.

Walke groundly,
Talke profoundly,
Drinke roundly,
Sleape foundly.

Of a lanthorne and light. 30.

A Lanthorne and a light mayde : manerly fayde.
But whiche to be light ? the Lanthorne, or the mayde.

Of a crie. 31.

Thou loftft a marke in iffews, criers cry.
Crie not fo for me crier, and marke this why.
I woulde rather geue thée a gowne of Tiffew,
Then be in dread to léefe my marke in iffew.

Of a watermans rowyng. 32.

Thy fares ouer the water thou fhouldft row them,
But vnder the water thou dooft beftow them.

Of tunge and witte. 33.

Thou haft a fwift runnyng tunge : how be it,
Thy tounge is nothing fo quicke as thy wit.
Thou art when wit and tounge in running contende,
At thy wittes ende, er thou be at the tales ende.

Of a peinter. 34.

Thou arte the painter of painters, marke who fhall,
In makyng and fettyng colours aboue all,

C iij   No

No painter, paintyng within Englands boundis,
Can fet fo fayre colours vpon fo fowle groundis.

Of Peter and Poll. 35.

I dwell from the citée in fubbarbes at rowles.
I pray to faint Peter to bring me nere Powles.
Alas, thou praift all in vaine, poore féely foule:
Peter will fet no hand, to bryng thée to Poule.

Of loffe of helth and wealth. 36.

How loft you your helth?
That glotony telth.
How loft you your welth?
That loft I by ftelth.
Who was your welthes wringer?
My thombe and my finger.

Of lookyng out. 37.

Stande in and looke out: hange out and looke not out.
Newgate and Tiburne, do bring both thefe aboute.

Of chafyng difshes. 38.

Wyfe, all thy diffhes be chaffyng diffhes plaft:
For thou chafest at fight of euery difhe thou haft.

Of hanging and ftandyng. 39.

Whether wilt thou hang vp with ropes of ynions?
Or ftifly ftande vp, with roperipe minions?
Forfooth, both for nomber and ftuffe truly caft,
As good hange with the firft, as ftand with the laft.

Of a mans head and the Pillery. 40.

Vpon the Pillery, your worfhipfull hed,
Vnto the pillery doth woorfhip far fpred.
Which woorfhip the pillery requitthe ill now:
For as you woorfhip it, fo it fhameth yow.

A prayfe of one. 41.

Se how fome aboue fome other, praifes win.
I praife thée for one thing aboue all thy kin.
They, without teachyng could neuer practife ought.
Thou canft play the knaue, and neuer was taught.

Of diuers bandes. 42.

All kindis of bands to be bounde in being fcande,
Headband, fmockbande, flaileband, houfeband, or hufbande,
Which fhall bind thée? not the laft on fea nor lande.
Before hufbands bands, in deuils bands I wil ftande.

Of couenantes. &c. 43.

Many pofis without appoficion.
Many couenantis without good condicion.
Many promifes without good payment.
Many arbitterments without good dayment.

Of promife and paiment. 44.

May I truft that he promifed?
Ye : fcantly to be performed.
Promifth he thrife or he once pay?
Somtimes he doth : but not alway.
Some thinges he promifth to pay euer.
Which thinges fo promifde he paithe neuer.

Of one that dare not fteale. 45.

Thou borowft, and thou begft, but when wilt thou fteale?
Neuer : for to be hanged fir I haue no zeale.
Thou wouldft fteale if thou durft : ye but I dare not.
Well then for thy hangyng, in this world care not.
And in the world to come, as well thou fhalt fpéede,
For good will to fteale, as thou hadft ftolne in déede.

Of the creation of the deuils dam. 46.

When was the deuils dam create, tholde withred iade?
The next leape yere after wedding was firft made.
In an ill time. when the deuill will that deuill die?
At that yeres end, that endth weddyng finally.

Of reward to a feruyng man. 47.

Wayte well : thy maifter will do for thée I wis:
Canft thou fpie nothing to afke of him? yis:
But when I afke, I can not haue that I craue.
No, afke him bliffyng : and that fhalt thou surely haue.

Who

Two properties of a feruaunt. 48.

Who fo that hath a good feruaunt, kepe him well.
Wel muft I kéepe thée then by this that I tell.
Singuler in many thingis : in this aboue all,
To take thy wages great, and make thy feruice fmall.

Of toughnes and tendernes. 49.

For toughnes and tendernes bothe in one man féene,
One like your mafterfhip few or none hath béene.
Axe ought of ye : then are ye fo tart and tough,
That your tauntis would touche a hors hart moft rough.
Giue ought to ye : thus tender and méeke are you,
Teares like Tares from your iyes, your knees to ground bow.

A queftion to a childe. 50.

Who is thy father childe, axt his mothers hufband.
Axe my mother (quoth he) that to vnderftand.
The boy dalieth with you fir : for verily
He knowth who is his father as well as I.
The man, of this childes wit, was wrapt in fuch ioy.
That he knew not what he might make of the boy.

Seekyng for a dwellyng place. 51.

Still thou féekeft for a quiet dwellyng place.
What place for quietnes haft thou now in chafe ?
London bridge. Thats ill for thée for the water.
Quéene hyth. thats more ill for an other mater.
Smartis Key. thats moft ill for feare of fmartyng fmart.
Carter lane. nay, nay, that foundth all on the cart.
Powles cheine. nay in no wife dwell not néere the chaine.
Wood ftréet : why wilt thou be wood yet once againe ?
Bread ftréete. thats to drie by drought thou fhalt be dead.
Philpot lane. that bréedth moift humours in thy head.
Siluer ftréete. Coper fmithis in Siluer ftréete : fie.
Newgate ftreete. ware that man, Newgate is hard bie.

Fafter

Faſter lane : thou wilt as ſoone be tide faſt : as faſt.
Crooked lane : nay crooke no more, be ſtreight at laſt.
Créede lane : they fall out there, brother againſt brother.
Aue mary lane : thats as ill as the tother.
Pater noſter row : Pater noſter row?
A gréede : thats the quieteſt place that I know.

Of three ſoules. 52.

Thou haſt three ſoules in charge : thy body ſoule one,
Thy féete ſoules twayne : but let thy feete ſoules alone:
Diſcharge thy body ſoule : and féete ſoules, poore elues,
They ſhall pay their owne fées and diſcharge them ſelues.

Of one ſaying of a hat. 53.

Sayd he that hat on his hed? nay : chaunce ſo led,
That by that time the hat cam he had no hed.

Of biyng a coate. 54.

I muſt bie a new coate for ſhame.
To get ſhame? nay tauoyde the ſame.
Tauoyde ſhame, thou maiſt deſire it,
But ten new coates will not hier it.

Of paryng neyles. 55.

Payre my neyles wife : nay man, if your neiles fayle,
Where can ye finde fréendes to ſcrat your ſcabd tayle?
Pare thine owne neyles then : for as they be led,
They proue féendly fréendes in ſcrattyng my hed.
That may be : but as thoſe woordes are ſoone ſpoken,
So euen as ſoone is a ſcald mans head broken.

Of a mans head. 56.

Thy head is great, and yet féemth that head but thin:
Without here without, and without wit within.

Of money in ones purſe. 57.

He hath in his purſe fortie or fiftie pounde.
Put *n* to *or*, and marke then how that doth ſounde.

Dd   The

Of freendes and foes. 58.

The deuill fhall haue fréendis : and as good reafon goes,
That the deuill fhall haue fréendis : as god fhall haue foes.

Of diffrence in fondry thinges. 59.

Small diffrence betwéene receiuyng and takyng:
Great difference betwéene maryng and making.
Small diffrence betwéene fighyng and fobbing:
Great diffrence betwéene baffyng and bobbyng.
Small diffrence betwéene fayre lookes and fayre woordes:
Great diffrence betwéene blount woordes and fharp fwoordes.
Small difference betwéene talkyng and tellyng:
Great diffrence betwéene fmartyng and fmellyng.
Small diffrence betwéene true loue and truftyng
Great diffrence betwéene rubbyng and ruftyng.
Small diffrence betwéene lowryng and fnowryng:
Great diffrence betwéene laughyng and lowryng.
Small diffrence betwéene wafte ware and wéedes:
Great diffrens betwéene good woordes and good déedes.
Small diffrens betwéene cloofnes and confealyng:
Great diffrence betwéene geuyng and ftealyng.

Of callyng one flebergebit. 60.

Thou flebergibet : flebergebet, thou wretche?
Wottft thou wherto laft part of that word doth ftretche?
Leaue that woorde or Ile bafte ye with a libet:
Of all woords I hate woordes that end with gibet.

Of crowes breedyng. 61.

I woulde wifh fome good prouifion to prouide,
That Crowes fhould neuer bréede by the hie waies fide.
They fo miftruft euery man to fteale their burdes,
That no man can fcape their opprobrious wurdes.
No man paffeth by, what foeuer he bée,
But thofe crowes be knaue him to the ninth degrée.
Should the crowes word ftand when he ragis and raues,
We fhould haue in England fortie thoufand knaues.

Thankes

Of Powles. 62.

Thankes to god and good people, Powles goth vp well:
Powles goth vp, but when goth poolyng downe : that tell.

Of a crowe keper. 63.

There be many cald crowe kéepers : but in déede
Thers no crowe kéeper but thou. in time of féede,
Where other kéepe crowes out, like fteruelinges forlorne,
To keepe crowes in plight, thou keepeft crowes in the corne.

Of Rape feede. 64.

Haft thou any Rapefeede ? ye : if you to rape fruite fall,
Here is Rapefeede : but thers hempfeede mixt withall.

Of red Rofes. 65.

What thinke ye worthe one buffhell of red rofes ?
More worthe then are two buffhels of red nofes.

Of Peniryall. 66.

I feeke Peniryall : haue ye eny ?
Séeke furder : I haue nother ryall nor peny.

Of Margerum. 67.

Haft any Margerumgentill ? ye in deede.
But it is fomwhat mingled with Nettilfeede.

Of Poppie. 68.

Lets fe Poppie feede : my Poppie feede is gone.
But for your grounde, I haue puppie feede alone.

Of Time feede. 69.

Haue ye any Time feede ? Time feede, ye be roode :
But it is fo miftimde, that it bringth no time goode.

Of Rue. 70.

I would haue a groatefworth of your feede of rew.
Ye fhall haue Rew feede inough, both olde and new.

Lyuerworte. 71.

What lacke you fir ? Lyuerwort feede I come to craue.
Lyuerwort I haue none : but Lipwort feede I haue.

Dd ij   Haft

Of pine appell. 72.

Haſt thou any graffes of the Pine appell trée?
Ye : pining graffes, great growers as can bée.

Of hartes eaſe. 73.

Haue you any hartes eaſe féede? ye for god, I.
But what other ware with harts eaſe will ye bie?
None : then haue I no harts eaſe for you brother:
We féede ſellers muſt ſell féedes one with an other.
To bie harts eaſe féede of me, that no man ſhall,
Except he bye ſome féedes of ars ſmart withall.

Of Parſnip ſeede. 74.

Here is Parſnip féede that will nip you as nere,
As ye were nipt with any parſnip this yere.

Of Anneſſe ſeede. 75.

This Anneſſe féede is browne : but to occupie,
Browne Annes as ſwéete, as white Annes like I.

Of lettis ſeede. 76.

I would bie lettes féede for my garden Ihone.
Lettes féedes? forſooth good maſter I haue none.
But put out *e s*, and theſe féedes Ile auow,
Beſt féedes in England for your garden and you.

Of good newes to a man. 77.

What newes? good newes for thée as wit can ſcan.
We haue newes that thou art an honest man.
Theſe newes comyng euen now thus freſh and new,
All men take for good : no man takth for trew.

Of least and moſt maſtrie. 78.

What is the leaſt maiſtrie thou canſt deuiſe?
Leaſt maiſtrie is a foole to wéene him ſelfe wiſe.
What is the moſt maiſtrie that thy wit ſpiſe?
The moſt maiſtrie is, to make a foole wiſe.

Of a man and a clocke. 79.

Men take man of earthly thinges moſt excellent:
But in one thing thou ſemſt vnder that extent.

A clocke

212

A clocke after noone aboue thee I avowe.
A clocke can go alone then : fo canft not thou.

Of a fpare horfe.　80.

Haft thou any fpare horfe to lend me one ?
A fpare horfe ? thers one : take him and be gone.
Sadled and brydled he was, and with that,
As the man leapt vp, the horfe fell doune flat.
He fell without helpe : but then vp to get,
Fyue men were to fewe him on foote to fet.
A fpare horfe (quoth he) the diuell may fpare him :
He that fhall occupie him muft bare him.
Sins this fpare horfe will not ferue the brother,
Yet of my fpare horfes hers an other.
Vp lept the man, hens ran the horfe amayne :
In ten myles galloppyng he turnd not agayne.
For iudgement in fpare horfe, let this be comparde :
Run euer, run neuer which may beft be fparde.

Of a hufband hangd.　81.

Is thy hufband hangd ? he was : but he is nat :
In fpyght of his foes I found fréends to eafe that.
For or my déere hart had hangd fully houres twayne,
I gat his pardon and cut him downe againe.

Of Horfadowne.　82.

Hyredft thou not this horfe at Horfadowne ? yis.
Where is Horfadowne ? that maift thou lerne by this :
In hye way, lowe waye, feyre way, foule way, féeld, towne,
Where fo euer this horfe is, there is Horfeadowne.

Of a Cocke and a Capon.　83.

A braue capon by a brag cocke late beyng,
The proud cocke thinkyng fcorne, the fame fo féeyng,
Sayde to the capon : what thou barren baftarde,
Perkft thou with me here as I were a hafkarde.
Where I, comely combed crowyng cockyng cock,
Am hufband or father to all this hole flock.

Dd iij　　　What

What (quoth the capon) thou lewde lecherous wretch:
Theſe chickens all for thine bendſt thou this brag to ſtretch?
As though there were but one treadyng cock alone,
Yes cocke yes : there be mo treadyng cockes then one.
But ſyns thou thus proudly doſt make this auaunt,
To repreſſe thy pryde, take this tale for a taunt.
I haue of mine owne : I treadyng hennes neuer,
As many chickens as thou, treadyng thy hennes euer.
This ſtrake the cocke in a déepe dumpe, dull and dead.
Hauyng a ſtyll toung he had a beſy head.
Two daies after this, he trode not nor fed not,
His comb ſore cut : but thankes to god it bled not.

Of diſdeigne. 84.
Iſt maiſtry to diſdeigne thinges by enuyſe ſcoole?
Nay nay, no more maiſtry then to be a foole.

Of Peter. 85.
Peter the proude, and Peter the poore, in whiche,
Poore Peter oft as proude, as Peter the riche.

Of one in Newgate. 86.
Art thou in Newgate to ſtand to thy tacklyng?
Nay : I am in Newgate to ſtand to my ſhaklyng.

Of ſauyng of ſhooes. 87.
Thou wearſt (to weare thy wyt and thrift together)
Moyles of veluet to ſaue thy ſhooes of lether.
Ofte haue we ſéene moyle men ryde vpon aſſys:
But to ſée aſſys go on moyles : that paſſys.

Of hogſtowne. 88.
The head man in hogſtowne, hogherd is expreſt:
Where hogis be pariſhioners, hogherd muſt be beſt.
Yet hogis head in hogſtowne is no Iohn a droyne,
Pigs dare not quich there, if hogis head hang the groyne.

Of coleprophet. 89.
Thy propheſy poyſonly to the pricke goth:
Coleprophet and cole poyſon thou art both.

Like

Of thinges vnlyke.   90.

Lyke wyll to lyke men fay : but not alway fo.
Contrary to contrary oftymes doth go.
When folke be moft open, their lowe parts moft lofe,
Then go they to ftooles that be made moft clofe.

Of the gentleneffe of a wyfe.   91.

Thy wyfe is as gentle as a falcon : trew.
And namely in this kynde of gentleneffe : Hew.
Beyng not hungry, lewre falcones when ye lift,
They wyll check oft, but neuer come to the fift.

Of catchyng a fly.   92.

A boy on his booke clapt hand to catche a fly :
Haft hir cryde his maifter ? nay god wot I.
Then thou fhalt drinke : maifter I haue hir I thinke.
If thou haue hir faide the maifter, thou fhalt drynke.
To furious maifters, what helpth fayre fpeeches :
Flies caught or not caught, vp go boyes bréeches.

Of a horfe wearyng great breeches.   93.

My horfe to weare greate bréeches is now afynde :
Why ? to kepe him from enterferyng behynde.

Of a recknyng at a fhotte.   94.

Geue vs a recknyng vppon this pot fyllyng :
What haue we to pay in all ? ten fhyllyng.
What comth our meate to ? foure fhyllyngs vp and downe.
Whatis drynke ? fyxe fhyllyngs : thats to fay a french crowne.
Why : haue we droonke more then we haue eaten, knaue ?
Ye, as many other men, many tymes haue.
Looke where fo euer malte is aboue wheate.
There in fhotte euer drinke is aboue meate.

Of vfe.   95.

Vfe maketh maiftry, this hath bene faid alway :
But all is not alway : as all men do fay,

In

In Apryll the Koocoo can ſyng hir ſong by rote,
In Iune out of tune ſhe can not ſyng a note.
At fyrſt, kooco, kooco, ſyng ſtyll can ſhe do,
At laſt kooke, kooke, kooke : ſyxe kookes to one ko.

Of one aſkyng for ſheepe. 96.

Cam there any ſhéepe this way, you ſheepiſhe maidis? nay:
But euen as you cam : there cam a calfe this way.

Of walkyng and talkyng. 97.

Walke thou narowly, walke thou néerely:
Walke as thy walke may ende chéerely.
Talke thou baſely, talke thou boldely:
In all thy talke, talke thou coldely.
Walke thou weatly, walke thou dryly:
In thy walke, walke not to hyly.
Talke thou meryly, talke thou ſadly:
Talke as thy talke may take ende gladly.
Walke thou dayly, walke thou wéekely:
In all thy walke, walke thou méekely.
Talke thou ſoftly, talke thou loudly:
In any talke, talke not proudly.
Walke thou fyrſtly, walke thou laſtly:
Walke in the walke that ſtandth faſtly.
Talke or walke oldly or newly:
Talke and walke plainly and trewly.

Of ſeeyng and feelyng money. 98.

Lackyng ſpectacles, canſt thou ſée money, Iohn?
Ye : but hauyng ſpectacles I can féele non.

Of takyng thinges wronge. 99.

Perſeyued and taken thinges right, thou haſt long:
But for one thyng in thee long ſens taken wrong,
Thy credite is toucht, and thou therby the wurs.
What thyng ſayſt thou haue I taken wrong? a purs.

A

Of a number of rattes miſtaken for
diuelles in a mans ſloppes. 100.

A byg breecht man fearyng a déere yere to cum,
Beſtowde in his bréeche a chéefe hard by his bum.
· And leauyng of thofe hofe for dayes two or thrée.
Rattes two or thrée crept into that bréeche they bée:
Poyntyng them felues of that chéefe to be kéepers.
In which ware watch be fure they weare no fléepers.
No wyght rydyng men : from Sandwich to Sarum,
Could wyn that chéefe from them without a larum.
At thrée daies end this man puttyng thefe hofe on,
Hauyng tyde his points, the rattis began anon
To ſtarte and to ſturre that bréeche round aboute,
To féeke and fynde fum way, what way to get out.
But that bréeche was bolſtred fo with fuch brode barres,
Suche crankis, fuch cony holes, fuch cuttes and fuch ſtarres,
With warde, within warde, that the rattes were as faſt,
As though they with théeues in newgate had bene caſt.
But this man in his bréech feelyng fuch fumblyng,
Such rollyng, fuch rumblyng, ioyſtyng and iumblyng,
He was therwith ſtriken in a frantike feare:
Thinkyng fure to him felfe that fome fprites were theare.
He ran out, he cride out, without cote or cloke,
Thofe rattes in thofe ragges whinde lyke piggis in a poke.
A coniurer cride he in all haſte I beféeche,
To coniure the diuell : the diuell is in my breeche.
Runnyng and turnyng in and out as he flung,
One of the rattis by the rybbes he fo wrung,
That the rat in rage to his buttock gat her,
She fet in hir teeth, his eyes ran a water.
She bote, he cride, dogs barkt, the people ſhowted,
Hornes blewe, bells rung, the diuell dredid and douted.

Ee   To

The fyxt hundred

To be in his breech to bryng him ſtreight to hell.
The wo and wunder wherof, to much to tell.
At laſt to ſée what buggis in his breech fraide him.
Foure or fyue manfull men, manfully ſtayde him.
The rattes hoppyng out at his hoſe pullyng of,
All this ſad matter, turnd to mery ſcof.
When he ſaw theſe rattes by this cheeſe brought this feare
Reioyſyng the ſcape he ſolemnly did ſweare,
That in his breeche ſhuld come no cheeſe after that,
Except in his breeche he weare ſure of a cat.

FINIS.

IMPRINTED AT
London in Fléeteſtrete
by Thomas
Powell.

Cum priuilegio.

APPENDIX.

VARIATIONS IN THE EDITION OF
1566.

Sig.	Page	Line	
A	1	20	ANNO chrifti *omitted.*
ij	4	12	For one of them thinke I to take out of hande.
iij	6	31	Sens that one will not, an other will,
	7	14	While betweene two ftooles, my tayle go to the grounde.
B	9	15	And will may wyn herte, herein to confent,
ij	11	18	Whiche is, whether beft or wurft to be to be ledde
iij	13	1	*The. vii. Chapiter.*
C	18	32	For he er this thought this beft to be.
iij	21	7	Ye Ales, of a good beginning comth good end.
	23	23	Whom in itching no fcratchyng forbere,
D	26	5	Like a pickpurs pilgrim, ye prie and proule
ij	27	16	Colts (quoth his man) proue well with tatches yll.
	30		My fifter in lawe, and mine owne brother,
E	33	11	But hakney men fay, at mangy hakney hier,
	34	16	And byr lady freend . nought lay downe, nought take vp.
	22		To win me the woorth of a draught of drinke.
F	41	8	Beggerly beautie, and reueld ryches take.
ij	44	5	What he woulde haue, his wife was fet
	22		And hir beggs baggeft into his bofom fwept.
	48	4	Thefe two paft, he fayd to me, whan ye will,
	32		Well amended (quoth I) whan ye both relent,
G	49	29	As tholde yewes. God forbyd wife, ye fyrft iet.
	50	9	On his part, to this yong wife did appeere.

Sig.	Page	Line	
G ij	51	5	I fee, you can not fee the wood for trees.
	52	4	As a lyke compare in tafte, chalke and chefe.
		28	At your handes . and let fall hir holde, than be bolde.
iij	53	17	Three maie kepe counfayle, if two be away.
H	57	24	Sometyme in feelds, fometyme in the woodes.
		29	What, a cat maie looke on kyng, ye know.
	58	18	Then haue ye his head vnder your gyrdell.
ij	59	11	If ye can hunt, and will ftand at recite.
		12	Your maide examine, maketh him open ftreite.
		33	Without proofe to his proofe prefent or paft.
iij	62	5	Not minding therby, to depraue your wit,
	63	26	And in mad ieloufy fhe is farre gon.
		29	The prouerbe faith, he that ftrike with the fwoorde,
		33	Reporteth for a trouth, to the mofte mifcheefe
	64	20	And than, that the eie feeth not, the hart renewth not,
I	66	19	But ye can not fee a blocke in your owne.
ij	67	25	Thus to ende all thingis be we leefe or lothe,
	71	3	Thou fareft to well (quoth he) but thou art fo good,
		12	Thou letteft euen flyp, lyke a waghalter flypftryng.
		27	And runth away with it, where eche man feeth,
	72	12	Sooth bourd is no bourd, ought that mirth doothe.
K ij	75	4	Than wolde ye mend, as the fletcher mende his bolte.
		29	I haue herde fome, to tell this tale not feelde.
	76	4	Ye ftumbled at a ftrawe, and lept ouer a blocke.
iij	78	14	I will learne, to ftop two gaps with with one bufhe.
		21	Ye like then better an ynche of your will,
		31	I could doo as muche with an hundred pounde now,
	80	8	This light burdeine in long walke welny tyreth me.
L ij	84	24	Found weddyng, for loue, as good onely to flee.
iij	86	17	(For vnhoneft termes (I truft) there none here foundes)
	87	24	A lowfe and flea.
	88	7	A herer of fermon.
M	90	27	Thicke heares and thinne wittes be pleyntee.

Sig.	Page	Line	
M ij	91	17	All that be dead, dide for lacke of wynde.
		25	Of a foxes forgeyng fo feat reafon?
		30	Betwene thefe hennes and yonde wethercocke
iij	93	26	A courfe with a greyhound at the hare in the feelde.
	95	21	But it was at leaft wynkt at, I hear of trowth.
N iij	101	7	And as for holy day, thou doeft breake none,
		33	Thou haft a fhrewde wit in defre to dwell,
	102	1	Thus in precepts, except thou cleere appeere
	104	6	Whiche were the beft choice, froft neuer, and fnow euer,
O	105	33	Made I a lie to thee? Nay (quoth he)
ij	107	24	*A loufe and flea.*
iij	109	17	*Of the woorde enough.*
	112	4	To ftrike and chime . 12 . two houres before noone.
		31	Claw wher it doth fmart, tikell, where it doth itche?
P	114	25	Ye: but we may far fooner leerne (quoth I)
	120	9	And to be as wife as thou I wot art,
Q ij	124	26	Of treadyng of a worme.
		34	Of mirth and wifdome.
iij	126	5	Of the foxe preachyng.
R	130	22	All thinke better take . 20 . poundes, then geue one.
iij	133	32	Better for byrdes, but for byrders not fo good.
	134	18	Thou art far paft fhame, fhame to thinke on.
	136	1	Store is no fore, yes, ftore may be fore.
		8	Yong fainte, olde diuell: thers mo of women kinde:
S	138	17	As good to play for nought, as woorke for nought:
		19	*Of peinted fheathe.*
ij	139	9	May haue a lyttle, ventryng is no fuch.
iij	142	29	But ftreight there comth, a carteweare, of good horfes by:
T ij	147	22	Meafure is a mery meane.
	152	35	But how may we be fure, that Malkin is one?
U	153	5	A fcabde horfe is good enough, for a fcabde fquyre.
ij	155	6	Not nowe, but we were made fey fo long a fpace.
		17	Yonge fooles, and olde fooles, eche other will difdayne.

Sig.	Page	Line	
X ij	164	7	*Of ſmaule and greate.* 234.
		10	*Of the keyſe.* 235.
Y	169	33	Hap catcheth and holdeth very few doles.
	170	33	*Of long ſtandyng.* 291.
ij	171	13	*Of ſmellyng.*
iij	174	11	Of the leaſt tittle . that can come in triall.
	175	15	Of diſagreement.
		20	Of louyng of a geeſe.
		28	Betweene dogges & deere.
Z	177	29	*Of aduiſe agaynſt mockyng.*
	178	11	*Of horſe.*
		34	I would be in both, for the places and ſtuffes,
ij	179	5	Galeries, gable endes, chambers, parlers, halles,
		9	And when by louce bityng, the legge itchyng,
iij	181	26	You may ſeeme you, your wyues father woonderfoole well.
	182	9	Whens come theſe glitteryng ſpanges? from much wanton.
		12	Whens come corne crooked toes? from ſhort ſhapen ſhoone.
	183	26	Like ſo, for thou lookſt lyke a newe hunted ſowe.
	184	1	*Of the cutter of purſlane.*
		6	So had he neede, for he ſtandth in mans els.
Aa	185	29	*Of wreſtlyng.* 41.
ij	187	6	For choyce of one two thynges, thou maiſt reioice?
		19	Sir, in deede the pate is the chiefe parte of a dawe:
Bb	193	4	Thoſe are one behinde and on eche ſide,
ij	195	35	Bb ij
Cc	202	5	Yet haſt thou the march hares made propertee.
iij	205	16	*Of lanthorne and light.*
		20	Thou loſiſt a marke in iſſews, criers cry.
		31	At thy wittes end, er thou be at thy tales ende.
	206	17	Newgate and Tyburne, do bring both about.
	208	14	Who is thy father childe, axe his mothers huſband.
		25	Smarris Key . thats moſt ill for feare of ſmartyng ſmart.
		26	Carter lane . nay, that ſoundth all on the cart.

Sig.	Page	Line	
Cc iij	208	30	Philpot lane . that breedth moiſt humours in the head.
Dd	209	22	Where can ye finde freendes to ſcart your ſcabd tayle?
ij	211	19	Haſt thou any Margerumgentill ? ye in deede.
	212	1	*Of a pine tppell.*
	215	9	Beyng not hungry, lewre falcons when he liſt,
		19	My horſe to weare greate breeches is aſynde:
	216	24	Talke and walke blainly and trewly.
Ee	218	6	All this ſad matter, turnd to a mery ſcof.

Spenser Society.

LIST OF MEMBERS.

ADAMS, George E., M.A., F.S.A., College of arms, London
Adams, Dr. Ernest, Anson road, Victoria park, Manchester
Addis, John, jun., Rustington, Littlehampton, · Sussex
Agnew, C. S., Mount street, Manchester
Ainsworth, R. F., M.D., Higher Broughton, Manchester
Aitchison, William John, 11, Buckingham terrace, Edinburgh
Akroyd, Colonel Edward, M.P., Halifax
Alexander, John, 43, Campbell street, Glasgow
Aspland, Alfred, Dukinfield
Athenæum, Boston, U.S. (per Mr. H. T. Parker, 3, Ladbroke gardens, Kensington park, London, W.)

BAKER, Charles, F.S.A., 11, Sackville street, London, W.
Bailey, John E., 11, Bloom street, Manchester
Bain, James, 1, Haymarket, London, S.W.
Baltimore, Peabody Institute at (per Mr. E. G. Allen, 12, Tavistock row, London)
Barker, Philip, 63, King street, Manchester
Beard, James, The Grange, Burnage lane, Manchester
Beard, Joseph, 4, St. James's terrace, Hyde park, London, W.
Bidder, George P., 131, Market street, Manchester
Birmingham Library (per A. Dudley, librarian)
Blackman, Frederick, 4, York road, London, S.
Bladon, James, Albion house, Pontypool
Boston Public Library (per Mr. H. T. Parker)
Bosworth, Rev. Joseph, LL.D., F.R.S., 20, Beaumont street, Oxford
Bremner, John A., Albert street, Manchester
Brooks, W. Cunliffe, B.A., Bank, King street, Manchester
Brothers, Alfred, 11, St. Ann's square, Manchester
Buckley, Edmund, M.P., Dinas Mowdwy
Buckley, Rev. William Edward, M.A., Rectory, Middleton Cheney, Banbury

CALLENDER, William Romaine, jun., F.S.A., Water street, Manchester
Chamberlain, Arthur, Moor Green hall, Moseley, near Birmingham
Chamberlain, John Henry, Christ Church buildings, Birmingham
Christie, Professor, M.A., Owens college, Quay street, Manchester
Coleridge, J. D., M.P., 6, Southwick crescent, London, W.
Collie, John, Alderley Edge, Cheshire
Collier, John Payne, F.S.A., Maidenhead
Cope, Captain Richard, Harboro house, Ashton-on-Mersey, near Manchester
Corser, Rev. Thomas, M.A., F.S.A., Rectory, Stand, near Manchester
Cosens, F. W., Clapham park, London, S.
Cowper, J. M., Davington, Faversham
Crewdson, Thomas Dilworth, 8, Cecil street, Greenheys, Manchester
Crooke, John, 45, Russell square, London, W.C.
Crossley, James, F.S.A., Booth street, Piccadilly, Manchester
Croston, James, King street, Manchester
Crowther, Joseph S., 22, Princess street, Manchester

DAVIES, Benjamin, Adlington, near Chorley, Lancashire
Davies, Rev. John, M.A., Walsoken rectory, Wisbeach
Davies, Robert, F.S.A., The Mount, York
De La Rue, Colonel, 122, Harley street, London, W.
Devonshire, His Grace the duke of, Devonshire house, Piccadilly, London, W.
Dodds, Rev. James, The Abbey, Paisley, N.B.
Downes, W. W., Bank, Nantwich

ELT, Charles Henry, 1, Noel street, Islington, London
Ewen, Miss Mary, 34, Plymouth grove, Manchester
Ewing, William, 209, West George street, Glasgow

FAIRBAIRN, Rev. James, Newhaven, Edinburgh
Falconer, Thomas, Usk, Monmouthshire, judge of County court, Glamorganshire
Feigan, John A., King street, Manchester
Fletcher, James Ogden, M.D., Lever street, Manchester
Fletcher, John Shepherd, Lever street, Manchester
Forster, John, Palace-gate house, Kensington, London
Fowle, W. F., Boston, U.S. (per Mr. H.T. Parker)
Fry, Danby P., Poor-law board, Whitehall, London
Furnivall, Frederick J., 3, Old square, Lincoln's inn, London

GEE, William, High street, Boston, Lincolnshire
Gibbs, Henry H., St. Dunstan's, Regent's park, London
Gibbs, John, Knightstone, Weston-super-mare
Gibbs, William, Tyntesfield, near Bristol
Gratrix, Samuel, 25, Alport town, Deansgate, Manchester ·
Green, Rev. Henry, M.A., Knutsford
Griffith, Rev. H. T., vicar of Felmingham, Norfolk
Guild, James Wylie, 3, Park circus, Glasgow

HAILSTONE, Edward, F.S.A., Horton hall, Bradford, Yorkshire
Halliwell, James Orchard, F.R.S., &c. &c., 6, St. Mary's place, West Brompton, London, S.W.
Hamilton, William, jun., Glasgow (care of Messrs. Jack and Turner, York street, Manchester)
Hamlin, Charles, 27, Virginia street, Glasgow
Hargreaves, George James, Davyhulme, Manchester
Harrison, William, F.S.A., Samlesbury hall, near Blackburn
Harrop, John, clerk to the Guardians, New Bridge street, Manchester
Hartford, Connecticut, U.S., Watkinson Library (per Mr. E. G. Allen)
Harvard College Library, Cambridge, U.S. (per Mr. H. T. Parker)
Hatton, James, Richmond house, Higher Broughton, Manchester
Hayes, Thomas, bookseller, Cross street, Manchester
Hayward, Thomas, bookseller, Oxford street, Manchester
Heard, James, Aytoun street, Manchester
Herford, Edward, coroner, St. John's street, Manchester

Heugh, Hugh, Portland street, Manchester
Heywood, Arthur H., Bank, St. Ann's street, Manchester
Hill, George, 68, Ingram street, Glasgow
Hitchcock, Samuel W., 546, Strada della Ponte, Florence (agent Mr. Bernard Quaritch, London)
Holden, Thomas, Springfield, Bolton
Hopwood, John Bentinck, Cambridge (per Rivington and Co., 19, Trinity street, Cambridge)
Howard, Hon. Richard Edward, Cross street, Manchester
Hunt, —, chemist, Salford

JACKSON, H. B., Basford house, Whalley range, Manchester
Jackson, John, Chancery place, Manchester
Jenner, C., Easter Duddington lodge, Edinburgh
Johnson, William, F.S.A., 2, High street, Eton
Jones, Herbert, 1, Church court, Clement's lane, London
Jones, Joseph, Abberley hall, Stourport
Jones, Richard, Temple bank, Smedley lane, Manchester
Jones, Thomas, B.A., F.S.A., Chetham library, Manchester
Jordan, Joseph, F.R.C.S., Bridge street, Manchester

KERSHAW, James, 13, St. Luke's terrace, Cheetham, Manchester
Kershaw, John, Audenshaw, near Manchester
Kershaw, John, Willesden lane, London

LANCASHIRE Independent College (per Mr. Joseph Thompson, Pin mill, Ardwick)
Latham, Henry, M.A., Clarendon press, Oxford
Leigh, Major Egerton, Jodrell hall, near Congleton, Cheshire
Leigh, John, Whalley range, Manchester
Lembcke, Professor, Marburg (through Williams and Norgate, London)
Leppoc, H. J., St. Peter's square, Manchester
Lingard, J. R., 12, Booth street, Piccadilly, Manchester
Lockwood and Co., 7, Stationers' hall court, London
Lumby, Rev. J. Rawson, M.A., St. Mary's gate, Cambridge

MACFARLANE John, Gas works, Manchester
Mackenzie, John Whiteford, 16, Royal circus, Edinburgh
Maclure, John William, Bond street, Manchester

Macmillan, Alexander, F.S.A., 16, Bedford street, London

Manchester Free Library, Campfield

Marsh, His Excellency George P., Florence (per Stevens Brothers, 17, Henrietta street, Covent garden, London)

Mouncey, G. C., Castletown, Cahill, Ireland

Murdock, James B., 33, Lynedock street, Glasgow

Muntz, George H., Grosvenor road, Birchfield, Birmingham

NAPIER, George W., 19, Chapel walks, Manchester

Neill, Robert, Northumberland street, Higher Broughton, Manchester

Newcastle-upon-Tyne Literary and Philosophical Society (per Mr. Lyall, librarian)

New York, Clinton Hall Library (per Sampson, Low and Co., London)

Nicholl, George W., The Ham, near Cowbridge, Glamorganshire

Nichols, George W., Augusta house, Rotherhithe, London, S.E.

OAKEY, John, jun., 172, Blackfriar's road, London, S.

Owens College Library, Quay street, Manchester

Oxford Union Society (per Mr. Thomas Harris, steward)

PAINE, Cornelius, Oak hill, Surbiton, Surrey

Palin, Captain, Police office, Manchester

Panton, Rev. G. A., 2, Crown circus, Dowanhill, Glasgow

Parker, H. T., Ladbroke gardens, Kensington park, London, W. *(Two copies.)*

Paterson, William, 88, St. Vincent street, Glasgow

Payne, J., 4, Kildare gardens, Bayswater, W.

Peace, Maskell W., Green hill, Wigan

Peel, George, Soho foundry, Manchester

Pocock, C. Innes, Rouge Bouillon, Jersey

Portico Library, Mosley street, Manchester

Priaulx, O. de Beauvoir, 8, Cavendish square, London

RADFORD, William, Withington, Manchester

Redfern, Rev. R. S., M.A., Acton vicarage, Nantwich

Rhodocanakis, H. H. the prince, Higher Broughton, Manchester

Riggall, Edward, 141, Queen's road, Bayswater, W.

Roberts, Lloyd, M.D., St. John's street, Manchester

Roberts, William, M.D., 89, Mosley street, Manchester

Robinson, Samuel, Black brook cottage, Wilmslow

Robinson, W. W., Oxford

Rogers, S. A., St. John's street, Manchester

Ross, H., F.S.A., The Manor house, Swanscombe, Kent

Royle, Alan, Hartford hill, Northwich, Cheshire

Royle, Peter, Lever street, Manchester

Rumney, Robert, Whalley range, Manchester

Russell, J. R., Glasgow

SAUNDER, J. Symes, Devon County lunatic asylum, Exminster, Exeter

Scott, James, The Lochies house, Burntisland, N.B.

Sewell, John C., 22, Kennedy street, Manchester

Sharp, John, The Hermitage, near Lancaster

Sheldon, S., Cheshire (per Mr. T. Hayes)

Shields, Thomas, Scarborough

Simms, Charles S., King street, Manchester

Simpson, Joseph, Fernacre house, Cheetham Hill, Manchester

Slater, Edwin, Market street, Manchester

Slingluff, C. B., Baltimore (per Stevens Brothers, 17, Henrietta street. London)

Smith, Alexander, 214, New City road, Glasgow

Sotheby, Mrs. S. Leigh, Leipzig (care of Mr. Goodman, 407, Strand, W.C.)

Sotheran, Henry, 136, Strand, London

Stephenson, David, Chapel lane, Sale, Manchester

Stewart, A. B., Glasgow

Stone, Edward D., Eton

Strathern, Alexander, Sheriff's chambers, Glasgow

Sudlow, John, Whalley range, Manchester

Suthers, Charles, Riversvale, Ashton-under-Lyne

Swindells, George H., 19, Ancoats grove, Manchester

TANNER, Thomas H., M.D., 9, Henrietta street, Cavendish square, London, W.

Taylor, Thomas F., Highfield house, Pemberton, Wigan

Taylor, Mrs. Tom, Knutsford, Cheshire

Thompson, F., South parade, Wakefield

Thompson, Joseph, Pin mill, Ardwick, Manchester

Thorpe, Rev. J. F., Herne Hill vicarage, Faversham, Kent

Timmins, Samuel, F.R.S.L., Elvetham lodge, Birmingham

Turner, Robert S., 1, Park square, London

VERNON, George V., Osborne terrace, Stretford road, Manchester

WARD, Henry, British museum, London

Washington, U.S., Library of Congress (per Mr. E. G. Allen)

Watson, Robert S., 101, Pilgrim street, Newcastle-upon-Tyne

Weston, George, 7, New square, Lincoln's inn, London

Weymouth, R. F., Portland villas, Plymouth

Whalley, J. T., 14, Marsden street, Manchester

Whitehead, Jeffery, 8, Moorgate street, London, E.C.

Wilbraham, Henry, Chancery office, Manchester

Wilkinson, M. A. E., M.D., 10, Lever street, Manchester

Wood, Richard Henry, F.S.A., Crumpsall, Manchester

Woolcombe, Rev. W. W., M.A., Ardwick, Manchester

Wright, W. Aldis, M.A., Trinity college, Cambridge

YOUNG, Alexander, 38, Elm Bank crescent, Glasgow